TOOLS

FOR THE SOFTER SIDE OF BUSINESS

Analytical models for addressing the
people-oriented aspects of business

To Jeff Walsh

with compliments,

Balaji

by Dr. Balaji Krishnamurthy

ISBN: 978-0-578-48636-9

Printed in the United States of America.

I've had the privilege of running more than a dozen businesses over the course of my career. And through those experiences, I've come to understand something: In business, there are "hard" subjects (often numbers-oriented) and "soft" subjects (often feelings-oriented). Finance and marketing, for instance, are typically viewed as "hard" subjects, while organizational and people matters are typically viewed as "soft" subjects.

Most business problems fall into one of those two categories. And those dealing with issues in finance and numbers are in luck: As business people, we have collectively amassed a number of analytical models for addressing these "hard" subjects. You've likely come across many of these in school, in your reading, in TED talks — accounting models like income statement and balance sheet, and economics principles like price elasticity of demand, for instance.

But because matters like leadership development and performance management are seen as having to do with intuition more than analysis, the business community to date has neither designed nor adopted much in the way of standard models to help you deal with them.

In short — few models exist to help us analytically address questions like, "do I have a toxic workplace culture?" and "what's the best way to confront an under-performing employee?".

Through my work with hundreds of senior executives in various industries, I have accumulated a set of Tools — models of thought — to think about and analyze different business situations, especially the softer subject matters. What these Tools do is make the soft subjects "hard," and therefore, easier to understand.

Tools are models of thought that help you navigate the people-oriented aspects of business as analytically as you manage the money-oriented aspects of business.

Within these pages are a compilation of the Tools I've developed and amassed over the course of my career. In the back of the book, you'll find a Tool taxonomy, organized by eight common categories of business and eight different roles of a leader, meant to help you quickly find Tools applicable to your unique business needs.

Most of these Tools are my own creation, often inspired by others in some intangible way. Some of them are directly adopted or adapted from the works of others, both personal colleagues and published authors. I hope these Tools will help you take a more analytical, structured approach to the "soft" subjects you encounter in life and in running your business.

Balaji Krishnamurthy

Contents

6   Abandonment

7   Ways to Abandon

8   Advice for Victims

9   Affinity Mapping

10   Amygdala Hijacking

11   Analysis of Investment Portfolio

12   Anchoring

13   Archetypes of Performing Employees

14   Bible Thumping

15   Black Swan

16   Book of Tricks

17   Bruce Tuckman's Model

19   Category of Meetings

21   Change Management

23   Change Table

24   Circle of Concern

27   Co-accountability

29   Coaching through Advocacy

30   Communicating Change: Mermaids and Alligators

31   Conversation Meter

33   Convictions vs. Conclusions

34   Convolution vs. Conglomeration

35   Crossing the Chasm

36   Deming's Model

37   Diminishing Returns

38   Disciplines of Market Leaders

39   Discretionary Effort

40   Earns and Turns

41   Empowerment

42   Enthusiasm Decay

43   Facts vs. Interpretations

44   Fear of Empowerment

45   Feature Creep

46 Five Dysfunctions of a Team
47 Five Functions of a CFO
48 Five Roles of a Board
49 Five Temptations of a CEO
50 Fixed Point Theorem
51 Focus through Exclusion
52 Foreground and Background Conversations
53 Forks in the Road
54 Four Frameworks for Leadership
55 Four Types of Leverage
56 Front of the Room vs. Back of the Room
57 Gallery Owner's Dilemma
58 Give and Take
59 Habit Energy
60 Hierarchy of Intangible Assets
61 Holistic Compensation Model
62 How Level is Your Playing Field
63 How Taut is Your Bungee Cord?
64 Implicit Assumptions
65 Income Statement vs. Balance Sheet
66 Inside and Outside
67 Intensity of Presence
68 Inverse Square Law of Conversations
69 Investment Criteria
70 Jack Welch's Formula
71 Law of Hazard
72 Law of Inertia
73 Levels of Commitment
75 Levels of Performance
78 Long Tail
79 Loyalty
80 Management Hierarchy
81 Managerial Discretion

82 McKinsey's 7S Model
83 Mind Those Qs
85 Nine Box Matrix
86 Nine out of Ten
87 No Pain, No Gain
88 One Hundred Questions
89 Open vs. Closed
91 Parking Lot Exercise
92 Performing vs. Engaged
93 Personal Assets and Liabilities
94 Power of the Means
96 Preference for Anonymous Harm
97 Pressure vs. Stress
98 Pricing Models
99 Principle of Externality
100 Prisoner's Dilemma
101 Progress Curve
102 Quadratic Law of Conversations
103 Quality of Revenue
105 Rational Choice Theory
107 Resignation Exercise
108 Riding the Waves of Culture
109 Risk Profile
110 Rogers' Diffusion of Innovations
111 Scope of Consciousness
112 Signature Loop
113 Simple Formula
114 Situational Leadership
115 Sixes and Nines
116 Socratic Conversations
117 Specific vs. Diffuse
118 Speed of Change
119 Start With Why

120 Stewardship
121 Strategy Busting
122 Stream of Consciousness
123 Supervisor/Subordinate Escalation
124 Talking Stick
125 Test for Transparency
126 Test of a Teaching Organization
127 The Theory of White Space
128 Three Bars of Integrity
129 Three Dimensions of Performance Reviews
130 Topgrading
131 Touchpoints
132 Two Dimensions, Four Cultures
134 Types of Conversations
135 Valuation of Companies
136 Value Stack
137 Video Tape Test
138 Well and Fence
140 What Value Do You Add?
141 Tool Taxonomy
149 Applicable Roles

Abandonment

Abandonment is the willingness to let go of your most favorite child, your long held positions.

It is the capacity to turn completely against your own views when the reality of the situation demands it. Imagine you've been fired, and a new leader has replaced you. She has no emotional attachment to any product or service. What is the first thing she would do? What would she get rid of and what would she keep?

Abandonment can be one of the most valuable, yet most difficult, tools to exercise. It requires pragmatism, and is often both an emotional and professional process.

Tool Taxonomy

Business Lessons
General Management
Marketing

Applicable Roles

Visionary
Preacher
Strategist

Ways to Abandon

> There are three ways to abandon your business after making the decision to do so.

1. ***Sell It Now.*** Your business is worth more right now than it ever will be in the future. Cash it out now because the value will only go down from here.
2. ***Cannibalization.*** If you have two businesses competing in the same market, they are competing for market share. It is possible that your overall business is better off with only one of these businesses. If this is the case, displace your original business so your new business will thrive.
3. ***Milk the Cash Cow.*** Get all the money you can out of the business, even though you are running it into the ground. Typically, this is a business no one will want to buy.

Tool Taxonomy

Business Lessons

Marketing

Applicable Roles

Visionary

Strategist

⊘ Advice for Victims

| Look around you.

Victims blame someone or something else for the challenges they face. When coaching a person to move out of their victim mindset, it is helpful to consider how he views the past, present and future.

- The victim cannot change the circumstances of the past. Instead, encourage him to recast past events in a positive light, drawing wisdom from past experiences.

- The victim is likely to have a pessimistic outlook for the future. Help restore hope by encouraging him to envision a future he would really like.

- Instead of allowing him to dwell on what he wishes the present were like, encourage the victim to face the present as it really is.

Tool Taxonomy

Human Behavior

Personal Growth

Applicable Roles

Teacher

Coach

Affinity Mapping

> This is a technique for bringing structure to an unstructured collection of thoughts and ideas.

It can effectively bring closure to brainstorming sessions by providing order to the ideas generated.

1. Record each idea on a separate card or sticky note.

2. Stick the notes randomly on a large wall.

3. Invite the participants to rearrange and group notes as they see fit.

4. Let the participants continue moving the notes around.

5. Allow participants to move notes multiple times, often back and forth.

6. Continue until movement dies down.

7. Give each grouping a descriptive name.

8. Look for some order and structure among the groups generated.

Tool Taxonomy	Applicable Roles
General Management	Strategist
Marketing	Coach

Amygdala Hijacking

> The amygdala, a gland in the human brain, controls your natural impulse to either flee a difficult situation or fight your way out it.

This primitive response, part of a highly evolved system, kicks in quickly – perhaps during a stressful situation at work, resulting in defensive or aggressive behavior. In that stressful moment, stop and evaluate your amygdala response. Are you getting anxious? Are you becoming defensive or do you just want to walk away? Has your amygdala hijacked you? Acknowledge these feelings and where they might be stopping you from finding a resolution.

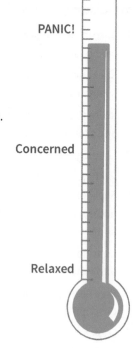

PANIC!

Concerned

Relaxed

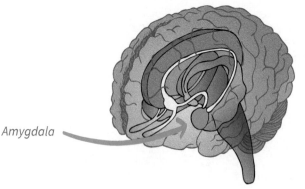

Amygdala

Tool Taxonomy

General Management

Human Behavior

Applicable Roles

 Coach

 Sergeant

Analysis of Investment Portfolio*

This tool helps measure your portfolio of existing or potential investment for diversified risk.

Create a graph, labelling the x-axis Level of Risk and the y-axis Value of Market Opportunity. Plot out where each investment falls and mark that point with a bubble, the size of which depicts the size of the investment. Once all your investments appear on the bubble chart, examine the patterns. If the points are well dispersed in various locations, your portfolio likely has a healthy risk variance. If the points are clustered together, your portfolio may lean toward an extreme – too risky or too conservative – and you may want to re-evaluate future investments. Large bubbles in the high risk zone might need to be examined.

*Adapted from Steven C. Wheelwright and Kim B. Clark – Revolutionizing Product Development: Quantum Leaps in Speed, Efficiency and Quality

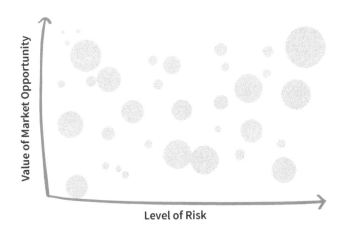

Level of Risk (x-axis)

Value of Market Opportunity (y-axis)

Tool Taxonomy

Business Lessons

General Management

Marketing

Applicable Roles

Strategist

Manager

11

⚓ Anchoring*

> Anchoring is the predisposition for a person to settle on the first presented option and compare all subsequent options to that first option.

It's difficult to evaluate objectively once anchored. When discussing options with a team, a manager should consider the four factors that influence a person's likelihood to anchor:

Mood. Depression or mental exhaustion can make a person settle with the first option as a means to end the conversation or decision more quickly.

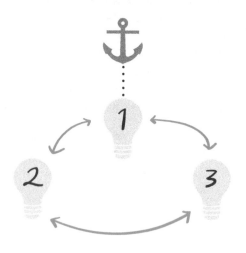

Experience. A veteran may use more caution and research when making a decision, while a novice may anchor quickly from fear or uncertainty. In contrast, more experience may lead a person to anchor onto that which is familiar, while an inexperienced person may be more open to new suggestions.

Personality. A strong personality is less easily influenced, but may also become enamored with a certain decision and refuse to move from it. A shy or insecure personality is much easier to sway, but also less likely to become stubbornly fixated.

Cognitive Ability. An intelligent, critical thinker is less likely to anchor on an option.

*Adapted from Richard H. Thaler
*Attributed to Daniel Kahneman and Amos Tversky

Tool Taxonomy

Human Behavior ▬▬▬

Marketing ▬▬▬

Applicable Roles

 Strategist

Teacher

Archetypes of Performing Employees

| What motivates an employee to perform well?

Understanding a high performing employee's motivation will help you be mindful of the circumstances under which his or her performance might degrade, and be intentional about addressing those situations.

Farmer. Steady, dependable and hardworking, but have minimal interests beyond work.

Hunter. Motivated by a prize or reward – financially, emotionally and with status. Always asking "what does that mean for me?

Soldier. Works hard and perseveres, but works for the fulfillment of a cause, not for personal glory or wealth.

Terrorist. Someone with a unique skill set that the company cannot do without. He knows his value to the organization, and will abandon accepted norms of behavior to fight the establishment. He does not (usually) mean harm, but feels downtrodden.

Tool Taxonomy

Corporate Culture

Human Behavior

Performance Management

Applicable Roles

 Manager

Coach

13

Bible Thumping

> Healthy organizations communicate well. As a leader, preach your message repeatedly, using multiple forms of communication.

Cascading Communication. Is your message pervading the office? Is that communication structured? This communication can be through emails, special events, posters, public praise to reinforce behaviors, etc.

Top Down Communication. Are you communicating your message directly to your employees? Are you taking the time to speak with your people, both in groups and one on one?

Lateral Communication. Are your managers acting as two-way communication channels? Managers should not just parrot the leader's message. They should also relay feedback, concerns and successes back to the leadership team.

Don't fear repetition. Messages need to be heard multiple times before they're properly absorbed. Repeated reassurances and displays that enforce the message add legitimacy and comfort.

Tool Taxonomy

General Management

Team Dynamics

Applicable Roles

Stategist

Coach

🦢 Black Swan*

> A black swan is an unusual event, a surprise outlier
> that creates an extreme and disproportionate impact
> in a certain field of study or within a certain group.
> t is often incorrectly rationalized after the fact.

When the phrase was coined, people believed black swans did not exist. The metaphor shows the fragility of any system of thought. In this case, observing a single black swan unravels all assumptions made in a system of thought that did not account for black swans.

In your business, consider:

1. What "impossible" occurrences have you not accounted for that could seriously damage or undo a certain project?

2. How quickly would you be able to change your thinking and adapt to new circumstances should a black swan enter the picture?

*Adapted from Nassim N. Taleb

Tool Taxonomy		Applicable Roles
Business Lessons	▮▮▮	● Visionary
General Management	▮▮	👥 Strategist
Marketing	▮	

 Book of Tricks

| Our strengths can manifest themselves as weaknesses.

For example, a leader with enormous energy who thinks and speaks quickly may intimidate a subordinate. The leader's dynamic presence is still a strength, but in some situations it hinders communication. Instead of mitigating the weakness (which would mitigate the strength as well), create a page in your book of tricks.

Your book of tricks is a compilation of ways to deal with strengths that manifests themselves as weaknesses in certain situations. The entries in your book of tricks suggest ways you might behave that would be more appropriate for the situation, even though it might be counter to your natural mode of behavior.

Tool Taxonomy	Applicable Roles
Human Behavior ▭	Teacher
Personal Growth ▭	Coach

⊞ Bruce Tuckman's Model*

As a new team comes together, it will progress through four development stages:

Forming. Members depend on the leader for guidance and direction. The team lacks agreement on their goals and lacks clarity on their roles. Members ignore processes and test the tolerance of the system and leader. The leader must answer lots of questions about the team's purpose, objectives and external relationships.

Storming. Decisions don't come easily. Members vie for position and challenge the leader as they attempt to establish themselves in relation to each other and understand their roles. The leader's vision helps solidify clarity of purpose. The leader must allow people to bump against each other, while still keeping the peace.

Norming. Agreement and acceptance forms among the team, and members respond well to leader facilitation. Roles and responsibilities are clear and accepted. Big decisions are made with involvement of the leader. Smaller decisions may be delegated to individuals or small teams within the group. Commitment and unity are strong.

Performing. The team is more strategically aware. It has a shared vision and stands on its own without interference or participation from the leader. There is a focus on over-achieving goals, and the team makes most of the decisions using criteria established with the leader. The team has a high degree of autonomy.

As the team moves through each step, the leader should be aware of what to expect and be as hands-on as each stage requires. If the team stalls in the storming phase and cannot move on, the leader should be prepared to reassemble the team and begin at the forming stage again.

Tool Taxonomy

General Management

Team Dynamics

Applicable Roles

Visionary

Manager

Tool
Continued

17

Bruce Tuckman's Model* continued

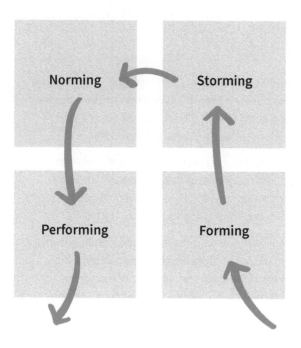

*Attributed to Bruce Tuckman

Category of Meetings

When chairing a meeting, most leaders employ an agenda framework, defining topics for discussion, time allocated, etc. Yet meetings consistently get derailed or run overtime. To address this, identify into which of four categories your meeting will fall: report, input, collaborative or decision. In all cases, the purpose of the meeting and what is expected of participants is clear, and the facilitator is held accountable for keeping things on track.

Report	Input
One way communication; speaker to audience	Speaker sets up; most of the communication is audience to speaker
Typically short; adhere to schedule	Short setup; adhere to schedule; overflow input through email
No action for speaker or participants	Action for speaker; no action for participants
Participants are expected to disseminate	Speaker is expected to assimilate

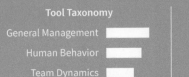

Category of Meetings continued

Collaborative	Decision
Collective collaboration; no closure expected	Collaboration and closure; clear decision-maker
More time consuming; speaker to summarize; stop promptly and reschedule as needed	
Action for speaker; no action for participants	Action for speaker and participants
All are expected to collaborate	All are expected to follow through on the decision

Change Management

When going through a major change, keep the following steps in mind:

1. Ask: Why are we changing?

2. Seek clarity on the impact of the change:
   - What is the timeline?
   - What is the process?
   - What is the scope within the organization?

3. Identify excitement and fears:
   - What are your personal feelings?
   - What are the opportunities/risks for professional growth/stagnation?
   - Hold an open dialogue about the organization.

4. Define the vision for the change.

5. Create a foundation for the change.

When the change is complete, measure success by asking:

1. Do you have a clear vision and goals?

2. Is there strong communication within the organization?

3. Is leadership engaged and involved?

4. Are people growing and learning?

Attributed to Keeley Hammond

Tool Taxonomy

Corporate Culture

General Management

Applicable Roles

Strategist

Manager

Tool
Continued

Change Management continued

Why are we changing?

Seek clarity on the impact
+
Identify excitement and fears
Duality of clarity and conflict

Define vision for the change

Creating a foundation
for the change

🛠 Change Table

Our relationships with change is defined by our comfort level, which generally falls somewhere within these six stages:

1. Some people are anxious of change and resist it.
2. Some people dislike change and avoid it.
3. Some realize change is inevitable and accept it.
4. Some see change as an opportunity and embrace it.
5. Some recognize change as a catalyst and invite it.
6. Some are energized by change and create it.

⣏ Circle of Concern

In any situation, our ***Circle of Influence*** is made up of all the things within our control – elements we can affect. The ***Circle of Concern*** contains all the things we care about – the things that concern us whether or not we can impact them. The gap between the two circles is our ***Donut of Worry***, the things about which we are concerned but have no influence. There are two ways to change the donut's size: shrink the circle of concern through communication, or expand the circle of influence through empowerment. Wisdom lies in understanding your circle of influence relative to your circle of concern and finding balance.

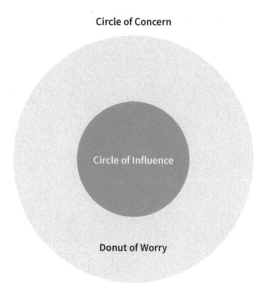

Circle of Concern

Circle of Influence

Donut of Worry

Tool Taxonomy

General Management

Human Behavior

Personal Growth

Applicable Roles

Manager

Coach

Donut of Worry – Glenn Mangurian Extension*

The **Victim** has a large circle of concern and a small circle of influence. He feels helpless and unable to change or control the situation. The result is paralysis.

The **Survivor** has a large circle of concern but a large circle of influence. He feels the world is full of challenges, but his hero mentality pushes him to overcome them. The result is burnout.

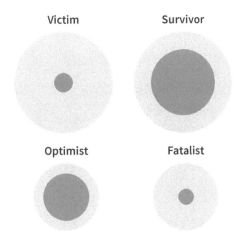

The **Fatalist** has a small circle of concern but a tiny circle of influence. His que sera attitude comes from a belief that the world's problems are not his problems, and that his worries will be resolved eventually. The result is a lack of stress but also a lack of motivation.

The **Optimist** has a small circle of concern and an equally small circle of influence. He sees very few problems. The result is a status quo mentality, but it should not come at the expense of ignoring reality. A healthy amount of worry can help motivate the optimist.

*In collaboration with Glenn Mangurian

Tool
Continued

Growing Your Nucleus

Your circle of influence is a living, breathing sphere.

Don't wait for someone to reset its boundaries; you can expand it.

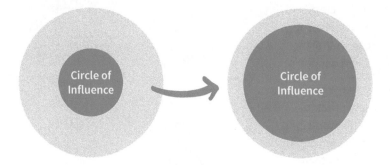

 Co-accountability

> The responsibility that a society/individual undertakes
> to hold people around them accountable.

Holding someone accountable for his or her commitments (or a lack thereof) is not a negative trait, though it's often misinterpreted as such. In a culture of co-accountability, employees feel comfortable holding each other to their commitments and will openly acknowledge when they failed in meeting their commitments. Those who keep silent when faced with a lack of accountability contribute to the deficiency. They share culpability with the delinquent.

Tool Taxonomy

Corporate Culture

General Management

Personal Growth

Team Dynamics

Applicable Roles

 Preacher

Manager

Sergeant

 Tool Continued

Co-accountability Triad

We often think about co-accountability in binary terms – the person who is offside (the delinquent) and the person who holds them accountable (the sheriff). Often there is a third person in the mix. The deputy or innocent bystander who can support accountability in the moment by speaking up on behalf of the sheriff.

The deputy is able to accomplish two things:

1. Their neutrality protects sociability. When the deputy simply points out an opportunity to exercise accountability, he/she bears some of the emotional weight of the exchange and protects the egos involved.

2. They provide a natural break in the conflict for a stop and teach moment. The deputy as a third party has the opportunity to raise awareness and open up the possibility for discussion.

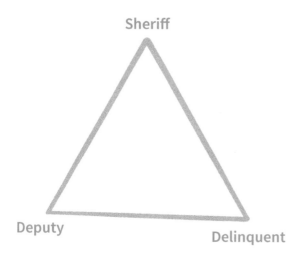

Sheriff

Deputy

Delinquent

Coaching through Advocacy

> This conflict resolution tool asks employees to
> advocate for a perspective other than their own.

Imagine a co-worker or direct report is complaining about another colleague
or situation:

1. Listen actively to what he's saying. Ask questions about the situation.

2. Give him specific ideas on what he could do differently – is he approaching the
   situation a certain way?

3. Ask him to play the other side – have him advocate for the person he disagrees
   with, while you advocate for his side. He must stay in character the whole time
   and genuinely attempt to convince you of the other perspective.

Tool Taxonomy

General Management

Human Behavior

Personal Growth

Applicable Roles

 Manager

Coach

29

Communicating Change: Mermaids and Alligators*

There are four potential mental states that exist when we think about making a significant change.

1. *The Prize.* The reasons why the future state will be good.

2. *The Alligators.* The problematic nature of the current state.

3. *Mermaids.* The benefits of the current state that you don't want to leave behind.

4. *Broken Bones.* The risks associated with making the change.

When communicating an upcoming change to a group, usually our goal is to get people onboard and excited about the bright new future. Of course, it is only natural to want to talk about The Prize and The Alligators. But don't forget the Mermaids and the Broken Bones still exist, because your audience sure hasn't. Pay tribute to the Mermaids and acknowledge the risk of the Broken Bones.

	Current State (status quo)	Future State
Perceived Benefits	Mermaids	The Prize
Perceived Risk	Alligators	Broken Bones

Adapted from Goldratt Consulting

Tool Taxonomy

Corporate Culture

General Management

Personal Growth

Team Dynamics

Applicable Roles

Preacher

Manager

Sergeant

Conversation Meter*

The conversation meter aims to create more authentic conversations by separating facts from interpretations.

It drives to a conversation that says, "Here are the facts as I understand them. And here is what I interpreted from those facts. Where did we disconnect, and how can we find a common interpretation?"

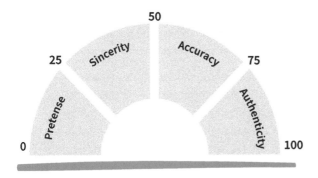

Tool Taxonomy

Corporate Culture
Personal Growth
Team Dynamics

Applicable Roles

Preacher
Teacher

Tool Continued

31

Conversation Meter* continued

Pretense. This type of conversation is simply for social gain or comfort – water cooler topics like the weather or a sports game. It's not about looking for facts or interpretations. Pretense conversations destroy value because participants agree to viewpoints they may not personally agree with for social gain.

Sincere. This type of conversation seeks the truth and is passionate, but the participants forget that all perspectives are true and impartial. Each participant allows his or her own passions to degenerate the conversation to the point where the sole purpose is to win. These conversations can actually be harmful to relationships, even if the motivation comes from a sincerely good place. The participants co-mingle facts and interpretations, though both parties speak with genuine passion.

Accurate. This type of conversation seeks the truth and separates facts from interpretations. The participants seek to resolve discrepancies in their facts. However, accurate conversations do not attempt to find a common ground between the two participants. They are good for getting facts on the table in a less emotionally charged way. Facts are aligned, but interpretations may differ.

Authentic. This type of conversation seeks the truth with accurate facts and an active curiosity and interest in both sides. Participants attempt to find a common view, aligning facts and interpretations.

*Attributed to Mickey Connolly and Richard Rianoshek, The Communication Catalyst

Convictions vs. Conclusions

Convictions are broad, encompassing statements with neither supporting nor contradictory evidence. They are statements of belief, fuelled by passion, and can often serve as the foundation for your organization's vision.

Conclusions are statements of deduction, supported by logic and reason. They are detailed assertions with substantial supporting evidence. Conclusions serve as the structure for your strategy, using logic as the rudder; the strategy is meant to complement the lofty and passionate vision.

Both convictions and conclusions are valuable in leadership. Draw a clear line between them, and be intentional about where they are used.

Both are statements about the future

Convictions

- Statements of beliefs
- Supported by passion
- Broad, encompassing statements
- No evidence to the contrary
- Serves as the foundation for your vision
- Passion is the fuel

Conclusions

- Statements of deduction
- Supported by logic and reason
- Specific detailed assertions
- Substantial evidence to support it
- Serves as the structure for your strategy
- Logic is the rudder

Tool Taxonomy

Business Lessons
Corporate Culture

Applicable Roles

 Preacher
 Teacher

⧗/⊠ Convolution vs. Conglomeration

Conglomerations are like a house of brands: they are large conglomerates that serve as a bank to a group of independent divisions. Employees identify as belonging to each individual divisions, not to the parent company. Divisions can each have their own culture and human resources. They operate as independently functioning beings.

Convolutions are like a brand house: they are integrated companies that freely share customers, vendors, employees and other resources between divisions. Employees identify as belonging to the parent company, not their individual divisions. The divisions each have a united company culture and community, despite working in different specialties.

Tool Taxonomy

Business Lessons

Corporate Culture

Applicable Roles

  Preacher

Teacher

34

Crossing the Chasm*

Moore's theory of crossing the chasm deals with how people adopt new technology. It divides people into a bell curve, split among five categories.

Innovators. These people are the leaders of a technology. They make up a very small portion of the market: those willing to take large risks to invest in new technologies.

Early Adopters. These are the drivers of a particular technology. With enough early adopters taking a risk, a product or technology is more likely to become common.

Early Majority. The technology has been refined and is now becoming accepted by the masses.

Late Majority. The technology has been established – these people are slightly late to the game, but are still catching the technology close to its peak.

Laggards. These people are embracing a technology that is already on its way toward being obsolete.

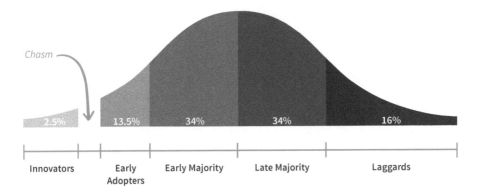

Chasm

| 2.5% | 13.5% | 34% | 34% | 16% |

| Innovators | Early Adopters | Early Majority | Late Majority | Laggards |

Attributed to Geoffrey Moore, Crossing the Chasm

Tool Taxonomy

Business Lessons

Marketing

Applicable Roles

Visionary

Strategist

⚏ Deming's Model*

The model identifies four types of people:

	Unconscious	Conscious
Competent		
Incompetent		

Unconscious competent. This individual is naturally gifted and gets by with little effort and little learning. He gets his job done without really knowing how. He doesn't need to study, prepare or expend much effort to be successful.

Conscious competent. This individual studies and prepares. He knows the precise steps it will take for his plan to be successful and he works hard to get it done.

The unconscious incompetent and conscious incompetent have the same behaviors as their competent counterparts, but with unimpressive results.

While things come more naturally and easily to the unconscious competent, the true benefit lies in being a conscious competent. If the situation or environment changes, both the conscious and unconscious competent will drop into incompetency. But the conscious individual already has a framework for getting himself back to competency. His *modus operandi* is to learn, research and plan, bootstrapping himself back to competency.

W. Edwards Deming originally developed this model for quality control in the automotive industry. He argued that to build a complex system, you must ensure each part of the system is a conscious competent. Similarly, successful leaders are intentionally conscious in all they do.

Adapted from the work of W. Edwards Deming

Tool Taxonomy

Corporate Culture ▬▬▬

Human Behavior ▬▬

Personal Growth ▬▬

Applicable Roles

Teacher

Manager

Diminishing Returns

All employees have unique contributions to bring to the team. Over time, the organization absorbs those unique values and adds them in some small part to the company's larger culture. At some point, all employees reach a point of diminishing return.

How then do the company and individual continue to benefit from each other?

1. The employee can learn new skills or specialties that allow her to contribute uniquely in new ways.

2. The organization can help place the employee in a new situation, within the company or outside of it, where she will flourish.

Tool Taxonomy

Human Behavior

Performance Management

Personal Growth

Applicable Roles

Strategist

Worker

Disciplines of Market Leaders*

> A market-leading company focuses its efforts
> and excels in one of three categories:

Operational Excellence. Focus on getting the customer the best value possible. Operationally excellent companies focus on efficient channels that result in the best value. Examples include Walmart, Target and Macy's.

Product Leadership. Focus on producing the most top-notch product on the market. Product leadership companies charge a premium for their superior quality (perceived or actual). Examples include Mercedes and Louis Vuitton.

Customer Intimacy. Focus on developing long-term relationships with clients and finding the best possible solution to all client needs. Customer intimate companies are focused on keeping the customer happy first and foremost. Examples include Zappos and Apple.

	Operational Excellence	Product Leadership	Customer Intimacy
Value Proposition	• Best total cost	• Best product	• Best total solution
Golden Rule	• Variety kills efficiency	• Cannibalize success with breakthroughs	• Solve the client's broader problem
Core Processes	• End-to-end product delivery • Customer service cycle	• Invention • Commercialization • Market exploitation	• Client acquisition • Solution development
Improvement Levers	• Process redesign • Continuous improvement	• Product technology • R&D cycle time	• Problem expertise • Service customization
Major Challenges	• Shift to new asset base	• Jump to new technology	• Total change in solution paradigm

Attributed to Treacy and Wiersema, Disciplines of Market Leaders

Tool Taxonomy

Business Lessons

General Management

Marketing

Applicable Roles

Visionary

Strategist

Discretionary Effort

> While all workers are expected to perform, there is a level of discretionary effort that is acceptable for an individual person.

A couch potato, for example, does very little – he sits around, never exercises, eats poorly. In contrast, an Olympic athlete exercises hard every day, follows a strict diet and often sacrifices personal time and relationships as she dedicates herself to training. Not everyone can be an Olympic athlete. To expect that level of effort from everyone would be unfair and unrealistic.

Each person falls somewhere on the spectrum. Identify how much discretionary effort you want to pour into individual activities, and aim to hit that level consistently. Be intentional about the level of discretionary effort you wish to invest in all of your activities, both personal and professional.

Where do you end up sitting?

Tool Taxonomy

General Management

Performance Management

Personal Growth

Applicable Roles

Preacher

Coach

Worker

⛁ Earns and Turns

> The amount of money a company makes is the product of its "earns" and "turns."

- A business focused on earns has high prices for quality items that don't turn over quite as often. A jewelry store, for example, sells very expensive diamond rings but might only sell a couple units per day.

- A business focused on turns has high turnover on relatively inexpensive items. A grocery store selling milk would be a good example.

The distinction between earns and turns becomes important when considering how to maximize profit. For example, would the grocery store benefit

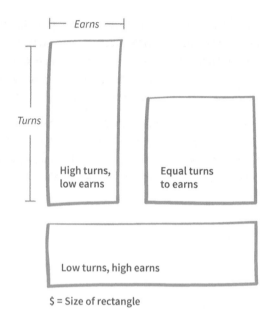

more from selling an additional 10 cartons of milk a day (increasing turns), or raising the price of each carton of milk by five cents (increasing earns)? Since its turns are already so high, it would be best served by increasing earns.

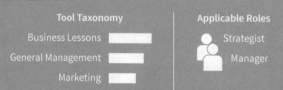

Empowerment

Allowing others to do as they see fit,
even if your opinion differs from theirs.

Empowerment is more than simply encouraging others to make decisions and take actions. A sign of true empowerment is when the actions of the decision maker differ from the inclinations of the manager, yet he is allowed to carry out the decision anyway. To test whether your employees are empowered, ask yourself: when was the last time a decision was made and supported that ran counter to the bosses' opinions?

Tool Taxonomy		Applicable Roles
Corporate Culture	�	
General Management	▬▬	
Human Behavior	▬▬	

Visionary

Preacher

Manager

41

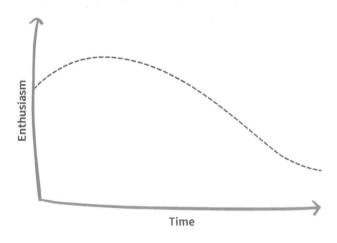 Enthusiasm Decay

At the start of a new project, team members' initial excitement often leads to high focus and output. Over time, enthusiasm will naturally wane as the new and exciting becomes the routine and ordinary. When undertaking a long-term initiative, give yourself a periodic "booster shot" of enthusiasm. Take a class, celebrate small successes, invite new people in to refresh your perspective and remind yourself of the end goals. Constant, small adjustments help keep enthusiasm high.

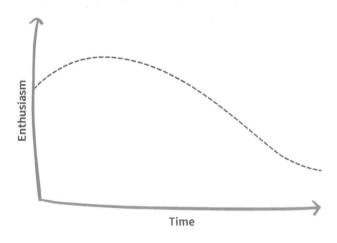

Tool Taxonomy		Applicable Roles
General Management	▮▮	Manager
Human Behavior	▮▮	Coach
Personal Growth	▮	

➡⇦ Facts vs. Interpretations*

> When two parties discuss differing opinions and struggle to come to an agreement, try breaking up their respective arguments into two segments: Facts and Interpretations.

By clearly stating the facts, you can find common ground that leads to an agreement. Facts are either true or false. Both parties are usually able to agree on the facts of the situation. Where opinions differ are on the interpretations of those facts. By first agreeing on the facts and then discussing the differing interpretations, you can find common ground.

**Adapted from Mickey Connolly and Richard Rianoshek,* The Communication Catalyst

Tool Taxonomy

Human Behavior

Personal Growth

Team Dynamics

Applicable Roles

Manager

Coach

ⓑ Fear of Empowerment

> Situation: Do you notice a lack of engagement in your employees? Do you feel you have empowered them, yet they don't feel empowered? This Tool helps you analyze and deal with that situation.

Model:

Leaders sometimes get in the way of employee engagement because they fear empowerment. Empowerment is a function of four behavior sets: responsibility, authority, accountability and transparency – RAAT.

Transparency
↓
Accountability
↓
Authority
↓
Responsibility

- *Responsibility.* As a leader, develop habits of mind to clarify the who, what and where of informal responsibilities, and promote those same habits of mind in your employees.

- *Authority.* True empowerment exists when we feel that we can make a decision that runs counter to our supervisor's intuition. Drive decision-making deep into your organization and give away that authority.

- *Accountability.* Support a culture where everybody holds one another accountable to their commitments, not only down the chain, but up the chain as well.

- *Transparency.* Have open, honest, transparent conversations about performance. Have the courage to talk about one another's shortcomings.

Possible Actions:

Start with transparency and work backwards. What can you make transparent in the organization? In particular, will the transparency you create cause an individual's lack of accountability to become transparent to all? When that happens, you can begin to part with authority and push decision-making deep into the organization. Promoting these four sets of behaviors creates a culture of empowerment and engagement within your organization.

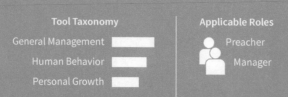

Tool Taxonomy

General Management

Human Behavior

Personal Growth

Applicable Roles

Preacher

Manager

 # Feature Creep

A common problem in product development, feature creep is the overloading of a product that was originally meant to stay focused and trim. Counter it by dividing all features into three categories:

Implicit Expectations. These are never stated by customer or vendor, but their absence would cause either serious annoyance to the client or harm the final product.

Differentiated Features. These set your product apart from its competitors. They should be few in number and clear in your communications. They should be featured in spec sheets, ads and promotions.

Unexpected Delight. The "wow" factor. These features are never stated nor promoted. As such, little monetary value can be gained for these features in the pricing of your product. However, this is how customers describe their experience, and this is what brings customers back to you. This is what makes them mention your product to their friends.

When designing a product, you should meet all implicit expectations, have a limited number of differentiated features to distinguish yourself and consider everything else to be unexpected delights. This thought process will force you to examine how many of the unexpected delights are worth including, given that you cannot charge for them.

Tool Taxonomy

Business Lessons

Marketing

Applicable Roles

 Strategist

Manager

Five Dysfunctions of a Team*

Organizations fail to achieve genuine teamwork because of five common pitfalls.

1. **Absence of trust.** Team members are unwilling to be vulnerable and open with one another about mistakes and weaknesses.
   - To overcome this, have the team share something personal from the past. Together, exorcise one undesirable behavior from the team.

2. **Fear of conflict.** Team members don't engage in passionate debate of ideas.
   - To overcome this, dig up buried disagreements and encourage everyone to say what they think. Embrace healthy conflict, addressing it and moving forward to the next challenge without any residual hostility.

3. **Lack of commitment.** Without open and unfiltered dialogue, team members silently dissent and never fully commit to decisions.
   - To overcome this, do not allow consensus in meetings and decision-making. Instead, separate fact from interpretation to uncover the best idea.

4. **Avoidance of accountability.** Without commitment, team members hesitate to call one another on counterproductive actions.
   - To overcome this, the team must embrace interpersonal discomfort. Communicate goals and standards, and reward co-accountability.

5. **Inattention to results.** Team members put their personal needs over the goals of the team.
   - To overcome this, make your recognition team-based and public, and share collective results publicly.

*Attributed to Patrick Lencioni, Five Dysfunctions of a Team

Tool Taxonomy		Applicable Roles	
General Management	▬▬	Manager	
Team Dynamics	▬▬	Sergeant	

46

Five Functions of a CFO

1	Accounting	Recording and reporting of financial transactions
2	Finance	The planning and distribution of business assets
3	Treasury	Management of cash, currency and long-term investments
4	Business Partnering	Partner to the business – helping them understand finance. Educating them on the ROI, margin changes, etc.
5	Investor Relations	Typically only necessary for larger organizations

Three additional functions that may or may not be included:

- Asset Management: Capital equipment, real estate and intellectual property
- Statutory Filings: Tax filings, regulatory requirements, etc.
- Risk Management, including insurance

Tool Taxonomy
General Management

Applicable Roles

Visionary

Five Roles of a Board*

| Eyes in, fingers out…

1. **Appoint.** Hire the CEO.

2. **Approve.** There should be a clear understanding of which sorts of decisions the board wishes to hold final approval. Commonly:
   - Policies
   - Operating and Strategic Plans
   - Major Balance Sheet Items
   - All Capitalization
   - Major Cash Movement

3. **Audit.** Are you following the policies and procedures put into place?

4. **Advise.** General advice and guidance with the understanding that there is no obligation for the CEO to follow.

5. **Advocate.** Representing and enhancing the reputation of the company they serve.

Designed in collaboration with Dennis Nerland

Tool Taxonomy

General Management

Applicable Roles

 Visionary

Five Temptations of a CEO*

1. ***Status over results*** – to overcome this:
   - Focus on results.
   - Publicly commit to measurable results.
   - Evaluate your success based on these results alone.

2. ***Popularity over accountability*** – wanting to be everyone's friend.
   To overcome this:
   - Hold people accountable.
   - Confront direct reports immediately about behavior and performance.
   - Clarify expectations up front to make confronting direct reports easier.

3. ***Certainty over clarity*** – having either too much certainty in yourself or too little, thus refusing to take action on a situation. To overcome this:
   - Provide clarity.
   - Set public deadlines for making key decisions.
   - Practice making decisions without complete information in less risky issues.

4. ***Harmony over conflict*** – wanting everyone to get along, avoiding conflict.
   To overcome this:
   - Establish productive conflict.
   - Draw out differing opinions and perspectives from staff members.
   - Engage in and allow passionate discussions about key issues.

5. ***Invulnerability over trust*** – wanting to be seen as infallible, fear of workers seeing you fail. To overcome this:
   - Build trust.
   - Acknowledge your own weaknesses and mistakes.
   - Allow direct reports to see your human side.

Attributed to Patrick Lencioni, Five Dysfunctions of a Team

Tool Taxonomy

General Management

Human Behavior

Personal Growth

Applicable Roles

Visionary

Preacher

49

Fixed Point Theorem

> However chaotic a transformation might seem,
> there is always a fixed point – an item of invariance.
> You cannot avoid leaving something unchanged.

People generally do not like change. When navigating through a difficult change or situation, identify the unchanging fixed point. By focusing on stability rather than change, you can provide comfort to the organization.

Tool Taxonomy

General Management

Team Dynamics

Applicable Roles

 Manager

 Sergeant

50

Focus through Exclusion

> Inclusion is easy – it makes people happy and appeals to the emotions, creating a sense of belonging. Exclusion is more difficult.

With your team, write 20 positive attributes about your company on a whiteboard, with a goal of narrowing the options down to five. Instead of choosing the five you like best, start by picking 10 attributes that you do not want in the final five.

The act of excluding options forces discomfort in the room. It causes you to think more rationally and to purposefully exclude those options that are good but not quite good enough.

Tool Taxonomy	Applicable Roles
General Management ▬	Preacher
Personal Growth ▬	Coach

Foreground and Background Conversations

> During any interaction, both a foreground and background conversation take place.

The foreground conversation is the overt, audible topic of discussion. The background conversation is the internal dialogue each person is having with him/herself. These are the silent thoughts that come to mind; they may or may not be relevant to the foreground conversation. Sometimes they provide valuable insight, extensions and connections to the topic at hand. Capturing your background conversations – writing them down – accomplishes three valuable things: it makes you intentional, makes those ideas actionable and helps make abstract material more concrete and applicable to you.

Foreground Conversation

- Audible conversation
- Involved parties: all physically present
- Sensitive to:
  > Social, cultural and political norms
  > How you appear to others and how others might judge you

Background Conversation

- A conversation with yourself
- Often judgmental of ideas, others and situations
- Sometimes irrelevant to the topic at hand, chasing a sequence of reminded thoughts

Tool Taxonomy

Human Behavior

Personal Growth

Applicable Roles

Visionary

Teacher

Manager

52

Forks in the Road

| Truly strategic decisions should be irreversible and controversial.

If most rational people would agree with the decision, it has become a *de facto* decision and merely tactical for implementation. When making a major strategic decision, leaders can be easily sidetracked by compromise or try to delay the final decision until everyone feels more comfortable. This is not good for the business, nor is it good for the decision-making team.

Strategic decisions must also be irreversible. It's tempting to "have your cake and eat it too," holding off committing to one path and keeping the alternative as a fallback.

Force discomfort by implementing a fork in the road technique: pick either Option A or Option B. If you choose A, could you reverse it later to B? If yes, the decision is not strategic. This decision should be hotly debated and controversial. If the answer is easy or self-evident, you waited too long to make the decision.

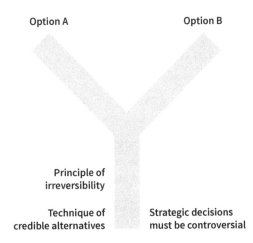

Option A

Option B

Principle of
irreversibility

Technique of
credible alternatives

Strategic decisions
must be controversial

Tool Taxonomy

Business Lessons

Marketing

Applicable Roles

Strategist

Manager

53

Four Frameworks for Leadership*

When approaching a situation, a leader falls naturally into four frameworks. There are situations where one approach is more appropriate than another.

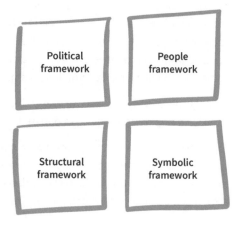

Political. This leader is an advocate whose leadership style is coalition and building. She is excellent at assessing the distribution of power and interests; she creates a network of ties to get what she wants. She uses persuasion first, negotiation and coercion only if necessary.

People. This is a servant leader whose leadership style is to support and empower. He is often visible and accessible; he tries to increase participation and move decision making down into the organization.

Structural. This leader is a social architect whose strengths lie in analysis and design. She is pragmatic and excellent at execution.

Symbolic. This leader is a prophet. He relies on inspiration, and views the organization as a stage or theater to play certain roles and give impressions. He frames experience with stories; he discovers and communicates a vision.

Attributed to Lee G. Bolman and Terrence E. Deal, Reframing Organizations: Artistry, Choice, and Leadership

---

Tool Taxonomy

Corporate Culture

Team Dynamics

Applicable Roles

● Visionary

● Preacher

⚒⚒⚒⚒ Four Types of Leverage

> Situation: In analyzing a business model, people often look at gross margin, operating margin and net margin. They are all measures of profitability. But it's also important to look at the amount of leverage the business has. Leverage is an indicator of how profitability can change with the growth of a business. This Tool points out the different types of leverage, which can help analyze how to increase profitability.

Model:

There are four kinds of leverage in a business.

1. *Revenue Leverage.* The idea of using the design, production or sale of the first product to sell many more with little effort. In other words, it's the ability to invest in assets that have the potential to generate high returns.

2. *Margin Leverage.* With increased volume, any fixed costs in the delivery of goods and services can be amortized over a larger revenue, providing margin leverage. In other words, with growth, you enjoy an improved gross margin.

3. *Operating Leverage.* Operating expenses should grow more slowly than revenue growth. A business that makes sales by providing a very high gross margin and fewer fixed costs has a lot of leverage. As the company grows, it finds itself needing to invest in people and systems to support the growth. Once the company is stable, you can expect operating leverage.

4. *Financial Leverage.* Using debt to acquire additional assets. For instance, putting $10 to work by investing $1 of your money and borrowing $9.

Possible Actions:

Look at each kind of leverage and examine if you can do something to increase it.

Front of the Room vs. Back of the Room

Front of the room leaders have a high intensity of presence. They are outspoken and express their opinions freely. They often "speak to think," forming their thoughts as they talk, and they draw energy from a crowd or audience.

Back of the room leaders are quiet, more thoughtful and careful not to express an opinion until fully thought through. They "think to speak," and express their positions sparingly. But when they express an opinion, it is considered and deeply held. These leaders expend energy when in front of an audience; it is not their comfort zone.

Both styles of leadership can be incredibly powerful and can complement each other. Each leader is more natural in one style than the other. By identifying your style, you can intentionally leverage your strengths and complement your weaknesses.

Tool Taxonomy

Human Behavior

Personal Growth

Applicable Roles

Visionary

Manager

▦ ▨ ▦ Gallery Owner's Dilemma

| What is in your gallery after a couple of years?

Imagine you own an art gallery and are responsible for buying, displaying and selling fine pieces of artwork. Over time, people come into your gallery and buy certain pieces, so you buy more artwork to fill the gaps. Once all the best pieces have sold, what are you left with?

In your organization, if you have an employee who for years has never advanced in his position and has not been promoted or sought after, is this the kind of employee best suited for his current job?

Cycle your people out – move your best people along and periodically get rid of mediocre workers who settle in the cracks.

Tool Taxonomy

Corporate Culture ▮▮▮▮▮

Performance Management ▮▮▮▮▮

Applicable Roles

 Manager

Coach

57

⌒ Give and Take*

| There are three personality types: givers, takers and matchers.

Givers have a natural inclination to give without expectation of gain. They are eager to help and to share credit. Givers can either be incredible team players or doormats, depending on how they are coached and treated in the workplace.

Takers sit on the opposite side of the spectrum. They seek to come out ahead in every opportunity and strategically ensure that happens. They often abuse givers and others in the workplace.

Matchers sit comfortably in the middle of the spectrum. Matchers give when they see potential in matching value. They strategically choose the people and situations to which they contribute, and seek to break even in just about every exchange. The majority of people in your workplace are likely matchers.

Attributed to Adam Grant, Give and Take

Tool Taxonomy

Human Behavior

Personal Growth

Applicable Roles

Strategist

Teacher

Worker

Habit Energy

| A deterministic world created out of random actions.

Our habits define and shape us. We build ourselves a deterministic world created out of random choices made under circumstances that have long passed. The presumption is that the deterministic world allows us to focus more of our energy and thought on more substantive matters. However, those very habits might be hindering us in today's circumstances. Find opportunities to question your habits and become intentional in choosing those of value.

Tool Taxonomy

Human Behavior

Personal Growth

Applicable Roles

 Coach

 Worker

▲ Hierarchy of Intangible Assets

In addition to the assets on the balance sheet, a company has many intangible assets. This list offers a hierarchy of the intangible assets of a company. The items at the top of the hierarchy are most difficult to create and hold the most value. They are also the most easily damaged. The items at the bottom of the hierarchy are the most easily transferred and difficult to destroy.

Brand. How your company is perceived in the marketplace, and the amount of equity that resides in your current brand.

Culture. The flipside of your brand; this is how your employees perceive the organization.

Channel. The access to and relationship with customers. The sales, marketing and distribution channels to which other companies may not have access.

Infrastructure. The ability to operate in the different geographies and locations in which you reside, with an existing legal, financial and business infrastructure.

Operations. The machinery and systems in place for all your employees to come to work and conduct the operations of your business every day.

Processes. Best practices or guidelines that your organization has developed.

Functional Excellence. The functional expertise that distinguishes you.

Evaluate your intangible assets with the following criteria:

- Difficulty to develop in terms of in time, money and energy
- Asset embodied in people (customers and employees)
- Ability to outsource or send it offshore

Tool Taxonomy

Corporate Culture

Team Dynamics

Applicable Roles

Visionary

Preacher

Holistic Compensation Model

When reviewing compensation packages in your organization, consider the liquidity and the time between contributions made and when each type of compensation is received.

Most organizations will have:

1. Life and Health Benefits
2. Incentive
3. Base Pay, etc.

Understand all of the composition vehicles you are offering your employees and make sure they are reasonably spread on this map.

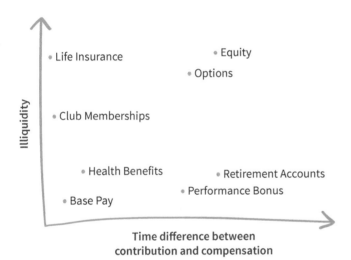

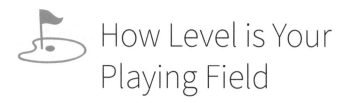

How Level is Your Playing Field

Historically, whenever a minority group has struggled to get a fair shake in society, social and economic data indicates they are under-represented in the distribution of opportunities in their society. As a result, there is a desire to use force fields to even out the playing field. A common example in the business world is the hiring and promoting of such minority groups. Business leaders are asked what they are doing about it, and your own position could be framed in one of four attitudes:

Indifference	You take the position that this is a social issue, not a business issue. Your place of business is the wrong place to address this social issue. Although you have a legal responsibility to not discriminate based on factors restricted by law, you have no legal or moral responsibility to address the larger social problem inherent in society.
Neutrality	You are absolutely neutral in your consideration. Being from that minority group neither hinders nor helps in your consideration of their candidacy. Your company diversity reflects the social and environmental sample you are selecting from.
Affirmation	You acknowledge the social and economic statistics and argue that it is in your best interest to ensure that candidates from that minority group are not overlooked. You resolve that your ultimate decision will be based purely on the candidate's merits, rather than the fact that they belong to that minority group.
Equalization	You acknowledge the social and economic statistics and self-impose a societal stewardship responsibility to help equalize this injustice. You commit to an increased level of representation, recognizing that it might lead to a less than optimal candidate at face value, but that it provides other value – both for yourself and the society – regarding minority representation.

Tool Taxonomy		**Applicable Roles**
Corporate Culture	▭	Strategist
Human Behavior	▭	Visionary
General Management	▭	Manager

←///→ How Taut is Your Bungee Cord?

Situation: As a leader, you are frequently called upon to create a vision, set a direction, establish goals and promote change. Many of these tasks place you well in front of the people you are leading, creating a certain amount of reservation, apprehension or even resistance. This Tool helps you understand, manage and work through this potential for conflict.

Model:

Imagine a bungee cord with one end held by your people, the other end held by you and the cord taut but not too stressed. Imagine that your proclamation of your vision/direction/goal/change is represented by you moving to a new place, presumably further away from your people, thereby creating tension in the cord – possibly significant tension. Your bungee cord is now very taut. This tension reflects the tension in the organization.

Possible Actions:

Here are some things you can do:

- You could move closer to your people, thereby reigning in your goal so as to be not so far out.
- One or more of your people could let go of the cord, leaving the tension to be borne by fewer people on that side.
- All of them could let go, sending you wheeling.
- The cord could break under the tension, leaving both you and your people wheeling.
- Your people can move a bit closer towards you, thereby reducing the tension.
- Explain these possibilities to your people and have them intentionally choose what they want to do.

Tool Taxonomy		Applicable Roles
General Management	▆	Preacher
Personal Growth	▆	Manager
Team Dynamics	▆	

# Implicit Assumptions

> Ask not: How do I solve the problem?
> Ask: What constraints have I assumed?

When solving a problem, we naturally bring implicit assumptions to the table. These unstated and often unconsciously-held beliefs about the situation can block transformative ideas. To deal with implicit assumptions, make them explicit. Compile a list of all the assumptions you are making, starting at the most basic and moving quickly to those most applicable to your problem. When you are free to question what you believe is "not allowed," you begin to find valuable solutions that might violate those implicit assumptions.

Tool Taxonomy

Human Behavior

Personal Growth

Applicable Roles

Strategist

Manager

Coach

Worker

64

🖩 Income Statement vs. Balance Sheet

This accounting tool can also be used when considering delegation of priorities and goals.

Income Statement Accomplishments provide value during one period in time (a revenue goal for a quarter or the completion of a client project, for example). These are best delegated to direct reports and people outside of the senior team, as they are usually well specified, measurable and provide instant gratification.

Balance Sheet Accomplishments provide value derived indefinitely into the future, until they decay or are destroyed. These decisions are best left to the senior team, as they are usually more difficult to specify and measure, and they provide long-term value with little immediate reward.

Income Statement Accomplishments

- Contributes to the income statement
- Value derived in one period in time
- Usually well specified and measurable
- Instant gratification

Balance Sheet Accomplishments

- Enhances the balance sheet
- Value derived forever in the future, until it decays or is destroyed
- Usually more difficult to specify and measure
- Long-term value with little immediate reward

Tool Taxonomy

General Management ▬▬

Performance Management ▬▬

Personal Growth ▬▬

Applicable Roles

Visionary

Strategist

Teacher

Inside and Outside

Gravitational pull vs. Repulsive push

This phenomenon is often seen between divisions of a company; it's the tendency of likeminded people working within a team to group together and bond. While at face value this team bonding is positive, it's important to consider an unintended consequence: the inward pull of those within the team creates a repulsive push for all of those who are not included. Counter the resentment that builds up by mingling insiders and outsiders. Ask them to positively acknowledge each other for contributions, and include non-team company members in team functions.

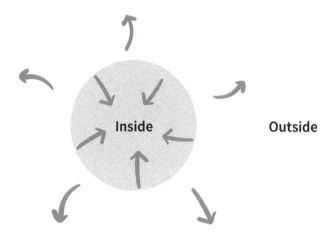

Tool Taxonomy
Corporate Culture
General Management
Team Dynamics

Applicable Roles
Visionary
Coach

Intensity of Presence

> When some people walk into a room, their presence
> – energy, enthusiasm, expression – is quickly noticed.

They voice their opinions with passion and conviction. Others are much more subdued, quieter. Their communication style is more considered and less expressive. Neither is better or worse – they're just different. Each individual has a natural range of intensity. It's important to recognize how your personal intensity, coupled with your level of authority in the organization, impacts those with whom you interact.

- People with a *low* power of authority and *low* intensity of presence may find themselves easily ignored or overlooked.
- People with a *high* power of authority and *high* intensity of presence can be very intimidating to others.
- People with *low* authority and *high* intensity, as well as those with *high* authority and *low* intensity, can be highly effective.

Understand your natural inclination and its outcome, then find a mechanism to help you adjust your behavior when needed. It can help you become more effective in your role.

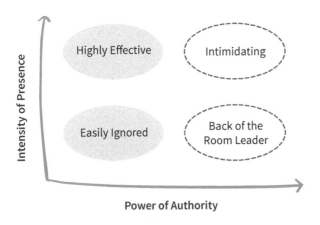

$\bigcirc^2$ Inverse Square Law of Conversations

> The amount of attention people deserve is inversely proportional to the square of the amount of attention they command.

It requires little effort to engage an outspoken person in conversation. These people are naturally expressive and require little prompting to voice their opinions. A person who does not command very much attention – someone who is naturally less vocal and more hesitant to share – requires more effort and encouragement when it comes to a discussion. These people are easily inhibited by the outspoken, and are less likely to voice their disagreement. This is not to say that either person's contributions are more valuable; the law is simply about the amount of attention required to elicit ideas.

Tool Taxonomy		Applicable Roles
General Management	▬▬	Manager
Team Dynamics	▬▬	Sergeant

RO👁 Investment Criteria

| When deciding whether to invest, consider four aspects:

Return on investment. The true criteria is the net present value of free cash flow. What are you likely to get back from this investment?

Investment cash capacity. This is a question of cash. Do you have the capacity to make this investment without significant risk to your current funds?

Acceptability of impact on income statement. This is a question of accounting. How significant will the impact on your income statement be to a board member or potential investor looking at your books?

Concentration of risk. Is this risk dispersed among various outlets, or is it concentrated in such a way that it might prove damaging?

Tool Taxonomy

Business Lessons

Marketing

Applicable Roles

Visionary

Strategist

69

Jack Welch's Formula*

| The best leaders have three traits: edge, energy and emotion.

Edge. They have a competitive edge; they want to win. They push to just about a breaking point before pulling back.

Energy. They have large amounts of personal energy, and spread it throughout their organization.

Emotion. They understand what makes their teams tick and are able to strike a balance between holding people accountable and keeping them optimistic.

Edge is what sets a leader apart. Many leaders master energy and emotion, but few can master edge.

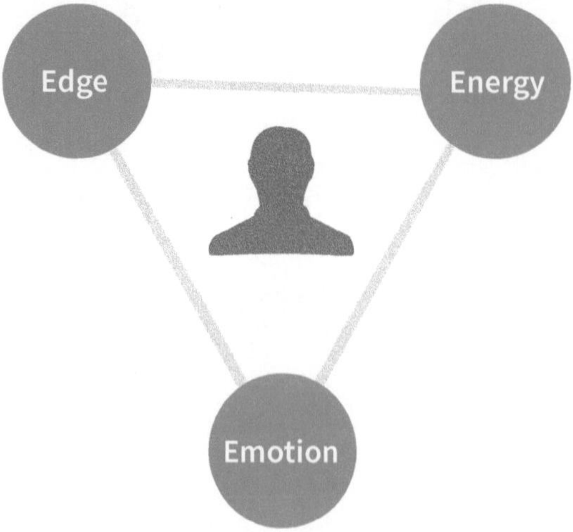

**Adapted from Jack Welch*

Tool Taxonomy

Business Lessons

Corporate Culture

Applicable Roles

Visionary

Preacher

◀ Law of Hazard

> All actions have both intended and unintended consequences. This is unavoidable.

The *focus of intent* is your desired action, ideally resulting in your intended consequences. The scope of impact is much larger than your intent and results in unplanned, unintended consequences.

Three ways **not** to deal with the Law of Hazard:

1. *Pretense.* Act as if you expected the unintended consequences to occur.

2. *Exhaustive search.* Before taking the action, analyze all possible unintended consequences and how you can mitigate them. (The result? Inaction thanks to analysis paralysis.)

3. *Rationalization.* Argue that the positive value of the intended consequences far outweighs the negative value of the unintended consequences.

Instead, recruit your naysayers to help you narrow the scope of impact to help minimize the unintended consequences.

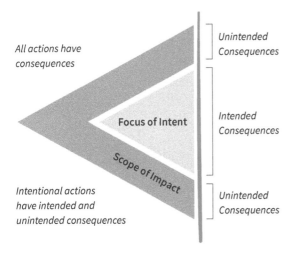

Tool Taxonomy

Business Lessons

Team Dynamics

Applicable Roles

Preacher

Strategist

 # Law of Inertia

> People tend to endure the pain of the present
> rather than risk enacting change.

The human mind is highly capable. In an instant, our minds calculate the pros and cons of both our current state and proposed future state. However, when we envision the changed future state and mentally assess the likelihood of those pros and cons, we give more weight to the probability of the negatives and discount the probability of the positives. Assuming the worst has helped us evolve to where we are today – our hard-wired response is to resist change.

To rationally overcome this, write down the pros and cons of both states and assign probabilities to each. This analysis forces you to be intellectually honest about the situation and move away from a fear-driven response to change.

Tool Taxonomy	Applicable Roles
Human Behavior	Preacher
Personal Growth	Strategist
Team Dynamics	

72

Levels of Commitment

| Change, Decision or Course of Action

1	**Ownership**	• I want "it" and will actively champion "it" to others. • I'm going to make "it" happen, even if I have to take some risks. • I'll renegotiate the boundaries if that's what it takes. • If I don't make this happen, I will see this as a personal failure.
2	**Stewardship**	• I want "it" and gladly accept a leadership role. • I'll do whatever I can within the boundaries that have been set. • I'll be disappointed if this fails because of others.
3	**Buy-in**	• I see the benefits of doing "it." • I'll gladly follow others to make "it" happen. • I am willing, at times, to do more than my share.
4	**Compliance**	• I won't oppose "it." • I will do what is expected, but no more. • I want to appear "on board" with "it."

Table continued on next page

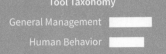

Tool Taxonomy

General Management

Human Behavior

Applicable Roles

Visionary

Preacher

Coach

Tool
Continued

Levels of Commitment continued

5	**Tolerance**	• It might be an "ok" thing to do or I may not see the point of "it." • If I have an option, I'll tell you I'll get around to "it" when I have time because it is not a priority for me right now. • If I don't have an option and you ask me, I'll tell you I am not on board with "it" but I don't want to lose my job over it.
6	**Resistance**	• I don't think "it" is right for us, and I might lose my job over "it." • I'll create roadblocks to "it." • I'll tell you I am not on board with "it" and will seek out others that are not on board.
7	**Departure**	• I think "it" is wrong and will leave if "it" happens.

Designed in collaboration with Glen Mangurian.

⊨ Levels of Performance

> Performance management seems to focus predominantly on non-performers. What about those who perform, but not as well as you once thought?

Selectable. An employee is said to be performing at a selectable level if her performance is such that, should her position become vacant and that employee be available in the market, knowing all you know about that employee, you would voluntarily select her to fill that position.

Incumbent. An employee is said to be performing at an incumbent level if her performance is such that, should her position become vacant and that employee be available in the market, knowing all you know about that employee, you would not select her for that position. But given that she currently occupies the position and there would be a cost associated with getting rid of her and with hiring a new employee, and taking into account the probability that the newly hired employee is going to be any better than your current employee, you conclude that it is not in your economic interest to let her go. In other words, the current employee maintains her position only because she is the incumbent.

Unacceptable. An employee is said to be performing at an unacceptable level if her performance is such that it is in your economic interest to expend the energy, time and cost to get rid of that person and find somebody else.

Most managers speak with the employee when she drops into the unselectable level, rather than when she drops into incumbency. What would happen if you had this conversation at the earlier stage? Either the employee internalizes the gravity of the situation and makes amends, or you shorten the time it takes for the employee to move from incumbent to unacceptable.

Tool Taxonomy

Corporate Culture ▮▮▮

Performance Management ▮▮▮

Personal Growth ▮▮

Applicable Roles

 Manager

Coach

 Tool Continued →

Levels of Performance continued

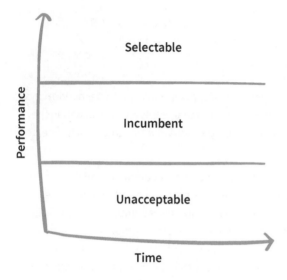

What Makes Someone Selectable?

Skills
What does the job description say?

Results
What are the expectations? The "what."

- Clear
- Objective
- Quantifiable

Behaviors
Do they follow the code of conduct? The "how."

⊤ Long Tail*

Paretto's Principle (the 80/20 rule) suggests that 80 percent of instances can be explained by 20 percent of causes. Zipf's Law, its antithesis, suggests that in certain situations there is a long tail (i.e. a small number of items do not account for a large number of instances). Take, for example, the million or so English novels. A bookstore could hardly carry 10,000 or so of the most popular titles. Yet, the remaining 990,000 titles represent a substantial market, not served by any bookstore – so observed Amazon. Many markets exhibit the long tail. Companies like Netflix, Airbnb and iTunes have taken advantage of such markets. Businesses that are able to take advantage of the long tail differentiate themselves by identifying niche markets and catering to them with more specialized offerings.

Histogram of Occurrence of Items

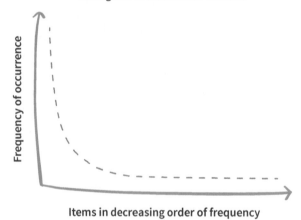

Attributed to Chris Anderson

Tool Taxonomy

Business Lessons

Marketing

Applicable Roles

Strategist

Worker

# Loyalty

> The practice of maintaining unrecorded items
> on the balance sheet of personal relationships.

Test for a loyalty-based culture: ask yourself, "Do we make management decisions that rational businesspeople would not?" Or, "Do your employees exhibit behaviors that go over-and-above what rational people would do?" In a loyalty-based culture, management and employees keep a mental balance sheet of IOUs. The underlying belief is that these unrecorded assets and liabilities will eventually even out. For new companies, the loyalty system is beneficial because it creates activity for which you do not need to spend cash. The trouble with loyalty is that it does not scale as a company grows. It becomes impractical (if not impossible) to keep track of the unrecorded items on the balance sheet of each personal relationship. For new employees, loyalty-based actions can become interpreted as favoritism. And when assets and liabilities do not even out, the faith that sustains the culture of loyalty dissipates.

Tool Taxonomy		Applicable Roles	
Corporate Culture	▬	● Visionary	
General Management	▬	●● Preacher	
Human Behavior	▬		

Management Hierarchy

There are a variety of different functions that a manager can operate in for business decisions. Depending on the size of your organization, you many find that your management has more or less levels.

Title	Future View	Function
CEO	>1 Year	**Policy and Procedure.** Determine what the company unequivocally stands behind. These are the fundamental policies of the organization.
Executive	</= 1 Year	**Strategy.** Set the direction of the organization.
Director	1 Quarter	**Process.** How we do things around here. The person is aware of how consistency in processes creates both efficiency and efficacy.
Operational Manager	1–3 Months	**Goals.** This person understands the goals of the organization and turns those into tasks that need to be done to achieve those goals.
Supervisor	1–3 Weeks	**Tasks.** Connect the tasks to the people who can execute. They will not necessarily decide what the tasks are, but they understand the workflow of the organization and can help facilitate the tasks be done on time and on budget.

Tool Taxonomy

General Management

Team Dynamics

Applicable Roles

 Strategist

Manager

80

≜ Managerial Discretion*

While hourly employees may clock in and out at precisely 40 hours per week, salaried employees often put in more than 40 hours if needed. These workers have managerial discretion to prioritize their work and schedule it based on the combined needs of the business and their personal lives.

There are privileges and obligations that come with this. Management has considerable discretion on the hours they keep, the quality of their work product and the scheduling of that work. However, they are expected to err on the side of higher quality when determining what is good enough. They are expected to work late, take work home or work evenings and weekends to ensure that critical projects are completed on time.

While the privilege gives managers a lot of freedom, the obligations impose a workload that adds up to more than 100 percent of their time. As someone rises in an organization, the privileges and obligations increase, resulting in greater disparity from 100 percent.

Execs
120% – 150%

Middle Managers
110% – 130%

Supervisors & Exempt Employees
100% – 120%

Hourly Employees
100%

Attributed to Steve Cobb, chairman, Henny Penny

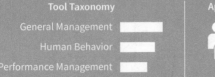

Tool Taxonomy

General Management

Human Behavior

Performance Management

Applicable Roles

Preacher

Teacher

Coach

McKinsey's 7S Model*

The 7-S Model breaks down organizational strengths into seven components. If all components are strong and working in harmony, there is a high chance that the organization itself is strong. The components are categorized as hard or soft skills.

Hard Skills:

- **Strategy.** The plans to build and maintain competitive advantage.
- **Structure.** The organizational hierarchy – who reports to whom.
- **Systems.** The daily processes and routines that staff members use to get the job done.

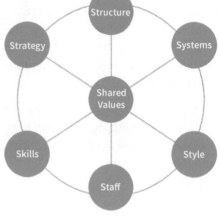

Soft Skills:

- **Shared Values.** Originally called "superordinate goals," these are the shared core values of the company. A company's "why," purpose and vision may also be included here. Shared values is placed in the middle of the model to reflect its central importance to the development of all other elements.
- **Style.** The style of leadership that an organization uses and promotes.
- **Staff.** The people who make up the organization.
- **Skills.** The unique skills and competencies of the staff and organization as a collective.

Use the 7-S Model to analyze your current company status or proposed future status and to identify gaps and inconsistencies between the two states.

Attributed to Robert H. Waterman, Jr., Thomas J. Peters and Julian R. Phillips, McKinsey & Company

Tool Taxonomy

General Management ▮▮▮▮
Marketing ▮▮▮▮

Applicable Roles

Strategist
Manager

ⓠ Mind Those Qs

| Would you like to hire intelligent people?

For most professional jobs, the answer is likely to be yes. What is intelligence? We offer a model to measure the various types of intelligence below.

Be intentional about the relative importance of each of the Qs in evaluating an individual for a specific position – how does the individual stand up in each of those measures? Make your own observations about KQ, SQ, DQ and MQ, but seek references on IQ, EQ, CQ, NQ, PQ and SQ.

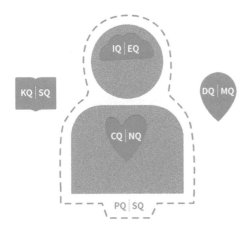

Tool Taxonomy

Human Behavior

Personal Growth

Applicable Roles

● Manager

 Coach

Tool Continued →

83

Mind Those Qs continued

Intelligence Quotient	An individual's ability to observe, comprehend, abstract, reason and deduce conclusions from structured information.
Emotional Quotient	An individual's ability to observe, comprehend, abstract, reason and deduce conclusions from human emotions and emotional displays.
Knowledge Quotient	An individual's knowledge (the amassing, retention and recollection of information) in a relevant discipline.
Skills Quotient	An individual's skill (the expertise in doing specific tasks, usually attained through years of practice) in a relevant discipline.
Diligence Quotient	An individual's diligence (the commitment to work hard, put the nose to the grindstone and get the job done) in a particular situation.
Motivation Quotient	An individual's motivation (the individual's drive to succeed, to accomplish and reach goals) in a particular situation.
Character Quotient	An individual's overall personal ethics (doing what is right).
Kindness (Niceness) Quotient	An individual's overall personal kindness (doing what is thoughtful and nice).
Personality Quotient	How an individual interacts with others (appearance, behavior, mannerisms, charisma).
Sociability Quotient	How the individual presents him or herself (interactions with others, the ability to collaborate and be a team player, individual's leadership capabilities).

Nine Box Matrix

> When thinking about your employees, consider two dimensions:
> Performance and Potential.

In other words, it allows you to separate the past from the future. Using this method, you can clearly see your top performers with growth potential versus poor performers who also lack potential. The challenge comes when evaluating the people who fall in the middle. It is possible to have a gem hiding in one of these boxes that hasn't had proper motivation.

	Poor	Good	Outstanding
High	Poor Performance, High Potential	Good Performance, High Potential	Outstanding Performance, High Potential
Moderate	Poor Performance, Moderate Potential (new role)	Good Performance, Moderate Potential	Outstanding Performance, Moderate Potential
Limited	Poor Performance, Limited Potential	Good Performance, Limited Potential	Outstanding Performance, Limited Potential

Leadership Potential

Performance

Tool Taxonomy
Business Lessons
General Management
Performance Management

Applicable Roles
Strategist
Manager

⬤⬤⬤⬤⬤ Nine out of Ten

| Imagine that you are the project manager for a 10-person team.

Your boss explores whether any members of your team hinder more than they contribute to the team's progress, and offers your team additional compensation – in exchange for letting one member go. Would you take the offer? If so, why was that 10ᵗʰ person on the team in the first place? Use this tool for keeping your team lean and efficient.

Tool Taxonomy		Applicable Roles
Corporate Culture ▐▬▬▬		Manager
Human Behavior ▐▬▬		Coach
Performance Management ▐▬		

86

No Pain, No Gain*

> Healthy conflict is an essential part
> of a transparent and honest culture.

Conflict falls on a spectrum. An ideal conflict point is constructive and does not step over the line to destructive. However, it's important to acknowledge that destructive conflict and offense is inevitable. Instead of fearing abrasive conflict, accept and manage it when it happens. Encourage healthy conflict by asking conflict-averse individuals to speak up, addressing problems and tensions as they arise and setting clear expectations.

**Adapted from Patrick Lencioni,* The Advantage
**Attributed to Alexis Kreml*

Conflict Continuum

Constructive
Destructive
Pretense Agreement
Ideal Conflict Point
Personal Attacks

Tool Taxonomy

Human Behavior

Team Dynamics

Applicable Roles

Manager

Sergeant

Worker

💬100? One Hundred Questions

| Write down the first 100 questions that pop into your mind.

This tool uses the Socratic Method (pg. 87) to help cut through mental clutter and bring the most pressing questions into focus.

In 15 distraction-free minutes, quickly write down 100 questions that come to mind. No answers, just questions. Once you're done, you'll likely find that the first third of the questions are very surface level (What should I eat for dinner?). The next third may be more existential (What is the meaning of life?). Focus on answering only the final 30 or so questions. These are the ones sitting deep in your subconscious. They will likely prove most difficult – and most valuable – to answer.

Tool Taxonomy

Human Behavior

Personal Growth

Applicable Roles

 Teacher

Coach

Open vs. Closed

This tool helps you become self-aware and intentional about areas in your life where you are committed or closed. Becoming "open" does not mean changing your position, but rather allowing yourself the possibility of considering an idea/person/scenario in future if necessary.

Closed Mind

- Ideas to which you are closed.
- Once you are aware that you're closed off to an idea, you are more likely to open yourself to the idea later. This allows you to consider the idea in light of new information or new circumstances.

Closed Heart

- People to whose ideas and very presence you are closed.
- You might have a very good reason for closing yourself to these individuals, perhaps rooted in past experiences. Being aware that you are closed to them allows you the capacity to re-examine your decision should the situation warrant it.

Closed Will

- A scenario to which you are closed.
- Your will is your internal disposition toward a situation or larger idea. While you might not like the thought of your life moving in this direction, remaining open to the prospect allows for future reconsideration.

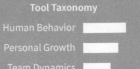

Tool Taxonomy

Human Behavior

Personal Growth

Team Dynamics

Applicable Roles

Preacher

Teacher

Coach

Tool Continued

Open vs. Closed continued

Open Mind

- Open to ideas that are new.
- Open to ideas with which you do not agree.

Open Heart

- Open to people that are new.
- Open to people with whom you disagree.

Open Will

- Open to situations that are new.
- Open to a future that seems uncomfortable.

Parking Lot Exercise

| You are in the parking lot!

Brutal or Compassionate? Imagine that, with a wave of a magic wand, you could let all of your direct reports go. They are now waiting in the parking lot. With that same magic wand, you could fill your newly available positions with anyone on the job market… or you could select members of your current team to rehire. Which would you choose? Which people would make it back into the building, and which would stay out in the parking lot? Now return to reality and consider: what will you do about the people you would have left in the parking lot? Do they know you wouldn't hire them back? Do they know why? This exercise forces you to examine your team and take action where it is needed.

Tool Taxonomy

Corporate Culture

Performance Management

Applicable Roles

Manager

Coach

Sergeant

⟨8⟩ Performing vs. Engaged

> We tend to value highly performing employees,
> but are we recognizing highly engaged employees?
> We often provide performance feedback, but how
> frequently should we give engagement feedback?

Performing employees give to get. They value what they get from the company, and it drives their effort. They give their best to the company in order to receive a good salary or other rewards and incentives. They could easily be lured by another employer from whom they can get more.

Engaged employees get to give. They love what they do. Their motivation comes from a deep pride and pleasure in the work – the rewards are incidental. They are more unlikely to be tempted by another employer from whom they can get more, but might well consider an alternate employer where they can give more.

Tool Taxonomy

Corporate Culture

Human Behavior

Performance Management

Applicable Roles

 Manager

Worker

92

Personal Assets and Liabilities

You begin a new job with a clean slate. You bring new ideas and skills to the company, and haven't yet built up any baggage from mistakes or habits. At this point, your asset to liability ratio is high.

Eventually you start to accrue liabilities. You experience failures, you form habits and you may get comfortable or complacent. At the same time, your capacity for bringing new skills slowly diminishes, even as you continue to learn. This is not due to incompetency; it's simply the product of time moving on. Over time, your asset to liability ratio will drop lower and lower.

How can you adjust this? Intentionally give yourself an asset boost or take a liabilities write-off. Write off liabilities by leaving the company or transferring to a different division. Boost your assets by learning new skills, taking on new responsibilities or seeking new ways to innovate in your company.

$\frac{\Sigma}{\Pi}$ Power of the Means

> Be careful when taking the mean (average) of multiple results. If you have a preference for a balanced effort, you might be better served by the ***geometric mean***, rather than the ***arithmetic mean***.

When evaluating performance across several different areas, it is common to calculate the mean in order to have a single value to assess and compare against others. The ***arithmetic mean*** is most commonly used, found by taking the sum of all the scores and dividing it by the total number of scores. This can be an inaccurate expression of the data, as it is easy for very low scores to go unnoticed when very high scores are present to compensate. As a result, this often leads to ***dumping***; intentionally allowing one or more areas to slide in order to excel in others.

To avoid this problem, consider using the ***geometric mean*** instead. Although the geometric mean might be a bit complex to understand, and an easy way to get to the same end goal is to view the arithmetic mean as being represented by the sum of the values and the geometric mean being represented by the product of the values. This is found by multiplied product of all the scores and then calculating the nth root of the product, where n is the number of scores being considered.

Arithmetic

Geometric

Example: On a performance management review, an employee is measured in three vital areas on a scale of one to 10.

Arithmetic Mean
(sum of the values)

Geometric Mean
(product of the values)

$\Sigma: \dfrac{4+8+9}{3} = 7$

$\Pi: \sqrt[3]{4 * 8 * 9} = 6.6$

$\Sigma: \dfrac{7+7+7}{3} = 7$

$\Pi: \sqrt[3]{7*7*7} = 7$

As is clearly visible in this example, the geometric mean provides a more precise calculation, and thus a more accurate representation of the data.

🧑‍🤝‍🧑 Preference for Anonymous Harm

> Humans have a higher tolerance for harm we cannot easily see than for obvious harm to named people.

While we reluctantly accept harm to a number of anonymous people (homeless people, for example), we do not accept harm to even a single named individual with whom we can relate (a kidnapped child, for example).

When it comes to your employees, how much anonymous harm will you tolerate? Managers often turn a blind eye to an irate or underperforming employee because they don't want to stir the pot. Yet how might the presence of that employee harm the performing, strong employees? Consider the risk of anonymous, silent harm in your employee evaluations. Don't wait to take action until people are being vocal about a particular employee or issue.

Tool Taxonomy	Applicable Roles
Human Behavior	Manager
Team Dynamics	Sergeant

⚡ Pressure vs. Stress

Tight deadlines, piles of paperwork, colleagues who asking for yet another "small favor"… We all experience these workplace pressures. Be aware of controllable pressures metastasizing into debilitating stresses that can affect work output and mental health.

Pressure is *the feeling of urgency caused by the necessity of doing or achieving something consequential or important, often within limited time. It can either turn negative or positive.* Positive pressure can give your employees an extra boost to finish a project or "thrive under pressure".

Pressure can also metastasize into stress, the state of mental or emotional strain resulting from adverse or demanding circumstances. **Stress is not caused by other people or external events, but by our own response to these pressures.**

How do you stop pressure from becoming stress? As a leader, help employees to first distinguish between the two and then invite them to reflect rather than ruminate.

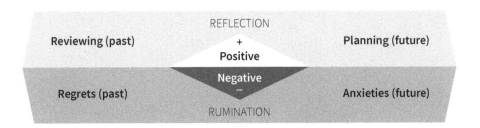

	REFLECTION	
Reviewing (past)	+ **Positive**	Planning (future)
	Negative −	
Regrets (past)	RUMINATION	Anxieties (future)

Adapted from "Rumination Nation." Wake Up, p. 6, https://bit.ly/2J1BeKZ
Attributed to Jay Holdnick

Tool Taxonomy

Performance Management ▮▮▮
Personal Growth ▮▮▮
General Management ▮▮
Human Behavior ▮

Applicable Roles

● Coach
Manager

97

 # Pricing Models

Intentionally consider the logic behind your pricing,
using one of four models.

- *Value-based pricing.* What value is the client getting from this product? What value are you providing the client as a service?

- *Margin-based pricing.* How much of a profit do you want to make from this product, based on what it costs you to produce it?

- *Competition-based pricing.* What is your competitor charging for a similar product, and how do you compare to that price?

- *Strategy-based pricing.* What is your strategy for pricing this product versus other products that the customer might buy as a result of this purchase?

Tool Taxonomy	
Business Lessons	
General Management	
Marketing	

 Applicable Roles

Strategist

Manager

Principle of Externality

In economics, externality refers to transfer
of value through means other than price.

This principle applies to products that gain more value as more people begin to use them. When a market exhibits this behavior, the market will grow exponentially. Examples of this include: the telephone, the internet and social media channels like Facebook or LinkedIn. In your business, can you identify any elements of externality that might fuel rapid growth?

Tool Taxonomy

Business Lessons

General Management

Marketing

Applicable Roles

 Visionary

Strategist

⚖ Prisoner's Dilemma

> Imagine this scenario: Two criminals are arrested; each is held separately with no means of communicating with the other.

The police don't have enough evidence to convict the pair on the principal charge, but they could get them both on a lesser charge. The police offer each prisoner a bargain: betray the other criminal (by testifying that the other committed the crime) and receive a lesser sentence.

	Prisoner B Silent	Prisoner B Betrays
Prisoner A Silent	Each serves six months	Prisoner A serves 10 years, Prisoner B goes free
Prisoner A Betrays	Prisoner B serves 10 years, Prisoner A goes free	Each serves five years

The game serves as a model for many business situations, particularly when it comes to pricing or competition. Two entities can often benefit from cooperating with each other, but may find it difficult, expensive or damaging to their pride to achieve that cooperation. Individuals make decisions to maximize what will be best for them, but in the end the whole market suffers.

Tool Taxonomy	Applicable Roles
Business Lessons	Strategist
General Management	Manager
Marketing	

Progress Curve

Many assume progress will happen at a steady, constant rate: a consistent linear upward momentum. In reality, progress will slow or halt all together – there may be challenges that set a company back or a sudden break that pushes it rapidly forward. When measuring a progress curve, it is typical for the mean rate of progress to be rather slow at first, and then rapidly accelerate after a certain point. Keep this in mind when making large corporate changes or moving through a difficult issue.

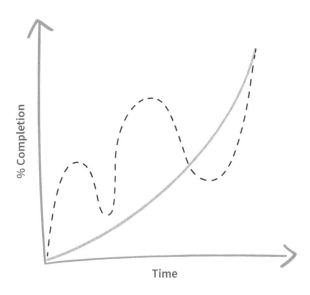

Quadratic Law of Conversations

When you have a group of people that need to be involved in a discussion, there are two ways you can go about it. You can either hold a single conversation that includes every person required, or you can have several separate conversations with just two people each.

Both methods have their benefits. A group conversation requires more organization initially, but greatly reduces the amount of time the discussion takes. Several pair conversations require less time organizing the meetings, but more time in the actual conversations. Mathematically, the amount of time spent in a series of pair conversations grows quadratically with the number of people involved in the conversations.

In addition, you must consider the integrity of the conversation. If the entire group is sitting at one table, everyone is more likely to leave with the same understanding of and takeaways from the conversation as everyone else. In multiple pair conversations, however, it is much harder to ensure that every person has a similar understanding, as each individual conversation is likely to (and perhaps necessarily must) change to accommodate the comforts of the specific people it involves.

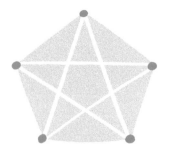

Tool Taxonomy

General Management

Human Behavior

Applicable Roles

Preacher

Strategist

Manager

Sergeant

Quality of Revenue

Situation: How do your customers/clients perceive the value you provide? Do they see you as simply assembling the raw materials and labor to produce and deliver the goods and services you offer? Or do they think you assemble and orchestrate this in an unusually valuable way, providing value beyond the actual work you did?

Model:

Quality of revenue is simply measured in terms of gross margin, or revenue less cost of goods sold. There's only so much room to bring down cost of goods sold, but how do you drive up revenue relative to cost? The answer is in your customers' value perception.

Value Perception

Brand Positioning
(what customers think of your company)

Product Positioning
*(how you package your product to make the
customer think of the product in a certain way)*

Market Positioning
*(selecting the kind of customers that are most
likely to find high value in your product)*

Tool Taxonomy

Business Lessons

Applicable Roles

 Strategist

Tool Continued

103

Quality of Revenue continued

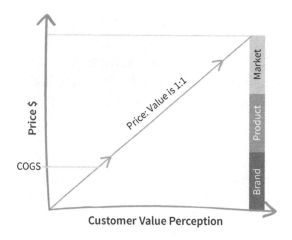

Possible Actions:

Consider what you might include or exclude from your total product to position it more attractively. Consider what kind of customers you want to go after, and make sure you aren't selling your product to the wrong customer.

Rational Choice Theory

> Most people behave rationally most of the time.
> However, any intermittent irrationality is usually due to a trap.

There are two systems responsible for our responses: the cognitive system and the dopamine system. The cognitive system controls our rational responses and allows us to think logically. The dopamine system, on the other hand, rides up our emotions and can sometimes keep us from making rational observations.

Because of how the two systems developed in the course of human evolution, the more advanced dopamine systems kicks in quickly, while the cognitive system is slower to respond. The dopamine system controls your behavior until the cognitive system can kick in. Depending on the situation and environment, the delay between the two can be significant.

Imagine you are looking to buy a house. After months of searching, you've found a house in a location you like and you're excited about the prospect of being a homeowner. As you tour the house, your excitement makes you gloss over some details. Cracked paint? Easy fix. Electrical wires hanging out of the wall? Adds character. A colony of mice in the kitchen? Well, you've seen Disney movies – mice can be cute. This is your dopamine system speaking. Over time, your dopamine levels will drop and give rise to the cognitive system. On your second tour of the house, in a more rational mindset, you're less likely to welcome an in-house mouse family.

When making difficult, emotional decisions, keep this in mind: Most people are rational, most of the time. They just need to be in the correct mindset.

Tool Taxonomy

Business Lessons

Human Behavior

Applicable Roles

 Strategist

Coach

 Tool Continued

Traps of Rational Choice: Emotional Response

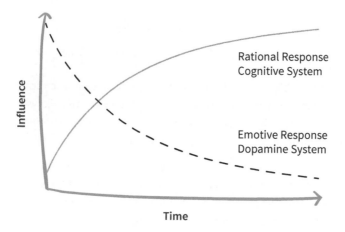

Traps of Rational Choice: Winner's Curse

How many pennies are in this jar?

⊨→ Resignation Exercise

> Imagine you send out a letter that invites your
> employees to submit their resignations.

You provide this caveat: if an employee submits his resignation and you do not
accept it, he will get a 20 percent bonus. However, if you do accept it, the resignation
will be considered voluntary and effective immediately.

To apply this to your workplace, gather your executive team and have them provide
a list of their employees. Explain the imaginary situation and ask them to discuss:

* What would each employee say when running into each other at the water cooler?
* Who would tender their resignations?
* Whose resignations might you accept?

Do not provide any directives for action, but ask the executives why they are
tolerating someone on their team who they would not be upset about losing.

Tool Taxonomy

Corporate Culture

General Management

Performance Management

Applicable Roles

Manager

Coach

⤳ Riding the Waves of Culture*

Culture is the way in which a group of people solves problems.

A problem that is regularly solved disappears from the collective consciousness and becomes a basic assumption, an underlying premise.

Attitudes to time. Certain cultures see time as passing in a straight line, a sequence of disparate events. Others think of time in terms of a circle or cycle. They may be more relaxed about time.

Universalism versus particularism. Universalists believe that what is good and right is very black and white. In particularist cultures, there are many more shades of grey – what is good may change depending on the obligations of certain relationships (such as friends or family) and unique circumstances.

Individualism versus collectivism. The individualist society values individual opinion and freedom of expression even if it disturbs the collective harmony of the collective norm. In contrast, the collectivist society encourages evaluation of the collective good, even if it imposes hardship or restrictions on certain individuals.

Neutral or emotional. In certain cultures, business relationships are typically all about achieving objectives. The brain checks emotions because these are believed to confuse the issues. In other cultures, business is a human affair and the whole gamut of emotions is deemed appropriate. Loud laughter, banging your fist on the table or leaving a conference room in anger during a negotiation is all part of business.

Specific versus diffuse. Specific cultures acknowledge the roles of each individual in the context to their position. In diffuse cultures, your status in one role diffuses into other roles – for example, in Germany, Professor Smith is treated with respect even by the butcher.

Achievement versus ascription. In achievement cultures, people are judged on what they have accomplished and on their record. In ascriptive cultures, status is attributed to people by birth, kinship, gender, age, interpersonal connections or educational record.

*Attributed to Fons Trompenaars, Riding the Waves of Culture

Tool Taxonomy		Applicable Roles	
Corporate Culture	▓▓▓		Visionary
Human Behavior	▓▓▓		Preacher
			Strategist

⚠️/💲 Risk Profile

When plotting the risk of an individual investment, counterbalance that risk with the possible return or reward that you stand to gain. Plot each investment on a graph with "Risk" on the x-axis and "Reward" on the y-axis. Ideally, the higher the amount of risk, the higher the potential reward. High risk, low reward scenarios should be avoided.

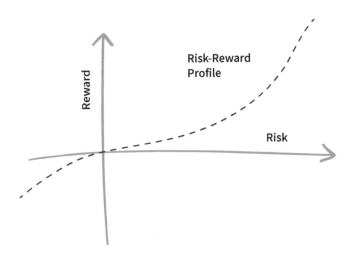

Risk-Reward Profile

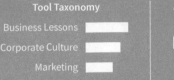

Tool Taxonomy

Business Lessons

Corporate Culture

Marketing

Applicable Roles

Visionary

Preacher

Strategist

Rogers' Diffusion of Innovations*

There are five stages of adoption for a particular product or technology: Awareness, Interest, Evaluation, Trial and Adoption. These are also sometimes known as: Knowledge, Persuasion, Decision, Implementation and Confirmation.

The rate of adoption is defined as the relative speed with which members of a social system adopt an innovation. It is usually measured by the length of time required for a certain percentage of the members of a social system to adopt an innovation.

Attributed to E. M. Rogers

Tool Taxonomy

General Management

Marketing

Applicable Roles

 Visionary

 Strategist

Scope of Consciousness

Unconscious perceptions are all the activities you do without really being aware you're doing them – you are able to act out of repetition or experience, almost without thinking.

Inside your **circle of consciousness** are all the things you know as well as those things you know you don't know. You can teach the things you know to others, and you can learn about the things you don't yet know.

The final circle is your **zone of oblivion**. These are all the things that you are not aware of – your blind spots, the unknown unknowns, all that you don't know you don't know.

Ask others to help you uncover what might be in your zone of oblivion, then develop tricks for expanding your circle of consciousness or managing weaknesses you uncover.

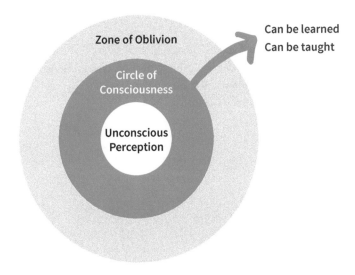

Tool Taxonomy

Human Behavior

Personal Growth

Team Dynamics

Applicable Roles

Visionary

Strategist

Coach

ℒ Signature Loop

It's common for businesses, particularly larger ones, to have a required signature hierarchy. Typically, someone is in the signature loop for one of three reasons:

1. *Adds value.* This person is knowledgeable about the issue needing sign off. She is likely to have a perspective that others do not, and likely affects the decision. This is typically evidenced by the fact that she declines her signature a measurable number of times.

2. *Intimidation.* This person represents authority and wants to make his subordinates seriously consider items brought to him for sign off. Although he might seldom, if ever, decline his signature, he argues that the need for him to sign provides enough of a filter.

3. *Reasons of ego.* This person is the superior, and thus she should automatically need to sign off on all items below her. For this person, signing off provides egotistical comfort.

You should only be in the signature loop if you fit into the first criterion: if you add value by being there. Notice that people in the first criteria decline a measurable number of times. Anyone who does not add value should be removed.

Tool Taxonomy

Corporate Culture

General Managemet

Applicable Roles

Visionary

Teacher

112

⊜ Simple Formula*

> The best leaders are constantly learning. How do you ensure that this education is disseminated throughout your organization?

Learn it. Study the problem or technique.

Live it. Make it real! Take every opportunity to intentionally use your new technique. Show others that this isn't a fad; make it an integral part of your routine.

Give it. Encourage others to use this new solution by actively teaching it to them and rewarding them when they use it properly.

Attributed to Jairek Robbins, TEDx Upper East Side

Tool Taxonomy		Applicable Roles
Human Behavior	▬▬▬	Visionary
Personal Growth	▬▬	Preacher
		Coach

Situational Leadership*

Hersey and Blanchard's model of situational leadership helps determine the best level of leadership involvement in a particular team, usually during its formation.

Telling. The team is immature and not empowered. The leader should focus on detached direction, telling the team the vision and what tasks need to be done in the day-to-day.

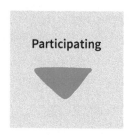

Selling. The leader should provide stronger direction, while allowing team members to begin stumbling on their own. The leader focuses on selling the vision to the team, acting as a preacher.

Participating. The team begins to normalize and function; a leader can now participate actively as a team member, while allowing his team to be empowered around him.

Delegating. The leader can now exercise detached delegation. The team is largely self-managing and ideally contains at least one potential leadership successor.

*Attributed to Hersey and Blanchard, Hersey-Blanchard Situational Leadership Theory

---

Tool Taxonomy

General Management

Team Dynamics

Applicable Roles

 Visionary

 Manager

•⟵⟶• Sixes and Nines

| Most performance review scores fall within a specific range.

While it might be rare for an employee to merit a perfect 10, rankings commonly land between seven and nine. To force yourself out of this rut, intentionally rate every employee as either a six or a nine – nothing in between. How many sixes are on your team? How many nines? Then deal with your sixes. Either discover what could turn them into nines, or let them go.

Tool Taxonomy

Corporate Culture

Performance Management

Applicable Roles

 Manager

Coach

🗨 Socratic Conversations

| Find a conversation partner, pick a topic and take a walk.

As you walk and discuss the topic with your partner, don't just provide your own input. Actively ask him: Why do you feel that way about this certain item? What if it were done this way instead – how would that change your feelings? Continue asking why; use the questions to force the other person to get down to the baseline of his convictions.

Tool Taxonomy

Human Behavior

Personal Growth

Applicable Roles

Visionary

Teacher

•/ ⚙ Specific vs. Diffuse

| Different people tend to speak with different levels of specificity.

People who are **specific** either expect that others will agree with them or tend not be concerned with disagreement. Their goal is to establish a very clear position and are often happy to take on (to understand or to challenge) opposing points of views. They will often express their opinions as statements of truth. (Example: "Coffee is best served at 180°F.")

People who are **diffuse** speak with less specificity so that all listeners can find some overlap in their position. They are more interested in finding common ground and then narrowing the common ground as far as possible, than finding the contrast between their true position and that of the other person. When they want to be specific they will often couch it as their opinion. (Example: "Coffee is best served hot.")

By becoming self-aware of your natural tendency you can be more intentional about how you speak in particular situations and with particular audiences. You might be able to structure your communication to balance your needs with those of your audience.

		Listener	
		Diffuse	**Specific**
Speaker	**Specific**	Assert & Consider	Assert & Evaluate
	Diffuse	Explore & Agree	Explore & Evaluate

⊂≡ Speed of Change

| What is your Limiting Factor?

1. Speed of Action

2. Speed of Risk

3. Speed of Trust
   - Alignment
   - Confidence

Tool Taxonomy

General Management

Team Dynamics

Applicable Roles

 Strategist

Manager

118

◉ Start With Why*

You can describe your business from three angles: your what, how and why. What do you do (your products or services)? How do you do what you do (your unique approach)? And why do you do what you do (your core purpose)?

While it's often easiest to identify the what and how – and it's what advertising tends to focus on – people truly connect with a company's why. If you can begin by defining your why, both corporately and personally, you will form stronger connections.

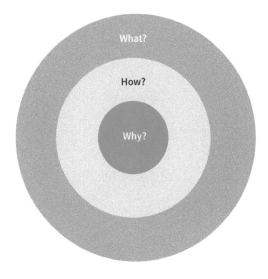

Attributed to Simon Sinek, Start With Why

Tool Taxonomy

Business Lessons
Corporate Culture
Human Behavior

Applicable Roles

Visionary
Preacher

 # Stewardship*

> Stewardship is the responsibility you have to protect, preserve and enhance assets that do not belong to you but have been temporarily entrusted to you.

It's one of a leader's most significant responsibilities. Your leadership style will be influenced by whatever you feel a strong sense of stewardship toward (your employees, for example). Acknowledge those items and become intentional about carrying out your stewardship responsibilities.

In collaboration with Glenn Mangurian

Tool Taxonomy		Applicable Roles
Business Lessons	▬	Manager
Corporate Culture	▬	Coach
Personal Growth	▬	

120

 # Strategy Busting

| This exercise helps critically examine your strategy for possible flaws.

- Divide your strategy group up into two teams: Competitor A and Competitor B. Remove the CEO/CFO; they eavesdrop but do not participate.
- Pick two of your real-life competitors, assign one to each team, and have the teams move into two separate rooms.
- Considering all you know about your company and your newly developed strategy, discuss:
  > What should Competitor A's (or B's) strategy be to compete against you?
  > How should Competitor A (or B) position you as they talk to your common customers?
- Encourage team members to immerse themselves in their roles, as if they were real outsiders to your company.
  > They should refer to their assigned competitor company as "our company."
  > They should refer to you by your company name.
  > Let them trash talk about you and your products/services (in privacy of the meeting room).
- The two teams come back together and report on their findings.

Walking through this exercise in good faith helps you understand the possible pitfalls of your strategy and plan accordingly.

Tool Taxonomy

Business Lessons

General Management

Marketing

Applicable Roles

Strategist

Sergeant

Stream of Consciousness

This exercise is meant to force you to be honest with yourself at a time when the truth may be hard to face.

Take 10 uninterrupted minutes and write down everything that comes to mind. Do not censor yourself and do no lift the pen from the paper. Later in the day or week, highlight profound thoughts or reoccurring worries. How can you address these?

Tool Taxonomy

Human Behavior

Personal Growth

Applicable Roles

 Strategist

 Teacher

122

⬈ Supervisor/Subordinate Escalation

> Suppose that you're a supervisor making a request of a subordinate. How should you approach them? Use the lowest level of escalation that will get the job done.

Establish a clear understanding of the words you use at each level – this can vary, based on how specific or diffuse your communication style naturally is, and your own intensity of presence. Make sure, however, that the force of your request is understood clearly.

Threaten. If you don't …

Insist. You should do …

Tell. I would like you to …

Ask. Could you please …

Suggest. Have you thought of …

Tool Taxonomy

General Management

Performance Management

Applicable Roles

 Manager

Sergeant

 # Talking Stick

This tool, borrowed from a native American tradition, helps bring focus and efficiency to meetings.

Choose an object to serve as your symbolic "stick" – a bean bag, a stress ball, something easy to throw or pass around. When having an intense discussion, only allow the person holding the object to speak. No one can interrupt her until she is ready to pass on the talking stick to the next speaker.

Tool Taxonomy

General Management

Team Dynamics

Applicable Roles

Teacher

Manager

Coach

124

# Test for Transparency

Model:

Test for when it serves to be transparent – when any one of the following are true:

1. Does this person have a need to know?

2. Does this person have a right to know?

3. Will it raise accountability in the situation?

Possible Actions:

Ask yourself who has a right to know and who has a need to know. When does transparency create accountability?

Need to know?

Right to know?

Raises accountability?

Tool Taxonomy

Corporate Culture

Human Behavior

Applicable Roles

Preacher

Manager

Coach

125

Test of a Teaching Organization*

| In a teaching organization, leaders develop leaders.

They believe it is their responsibility; there is a desire and an obligation to do so. It is what drives the organization. And it goes beyond simply investing time and resources into employee education.

The test:

- Do leaders take responsibility to develop others?
- Do leaders have teachable points of view?
- Do leaders embody those POVs in living stories?
- Do the employees spend 10 percent of their time teaching and 10 percent learning?

*Attributed to Noel Tichy, The Leadership Engine, "Winning Organizations are Teaching Organizations"

Tool Taxonomy		Applicable Roles
Corporate Culture		Visionary
Personal Growth		Teacher

◯ The Theory of White Space*

Situation: In a growing business, there is much to do, and the talents of the team aren't always a perfect match for the work. When the company is small, people reach outside their competency to fill in the gaps. As the company grows, however, it needs to shed that behavior. This Tool provides a way of thinking about this.

Model:

- These people are then less effective at both their extra work and their core work (which gets less attention).
- Filling the white spaces with new people allows the existing employees to focus back on their core.
- However, the shape of the work to be done is always changing, so the white space is dynamic.

Possible Actions:

Understand the white space being filled by new employees, and its overlap with existing employees who have "filled in." Be overt and intentional about the re-allocation of white space.

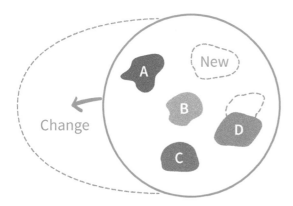

*Attributed to John Yerger

≡ Three Bars of Integrity

| The notion of integrity is often poorly defined.

This tool provides context for teaching what it means to act with integrity. The first and base-level bar of integrity is honesty: ***Tell the truth.*** It applies to all people, all of the time. The second and middle bar involves personal accountability: ***Do as you say.*** Most people abide by this some of the time. The third and highest bar of integrity is about transparency: ***Say as you think.*** Some people do this, some of the time. The art behind the third bar is to speak and act with compassion.

High Bar: Say As You Think   Some people, some of the time

_____

Middle Bar: Do As You Say   Most people, some of the time

_____

Base Bar: Honesty   All people, all of the time

_____

Three Dimensions of Performance Reviews

| Candid performance reviews are not just an opportunity, but an obligation.

Consider this model for written performance appraisals:

1. **Results.** The employee's accomplishments over the past year. This should speak to what happened, not what the individual is capable of. This can be grouped into **promised and delivered**, **promised and failed to fully deliver** and **unplanned but delivered**.

2. **Skills.** An assessment of the employee's natural skills and abilities, as related to the employee's assigned job or potential future assignments. This is like the tangible items on the employee's balance sheet, both the **assets** and **liabilities**.

3. **Style.** An assessment of the employee's interactions with the environment. Unlike **skills**, which can be demonstrated, **style** is a bit more difficult to establish unequivocally.

Results *Income Statement View*	Promised and delivered
	Promised and failed to fully deliver
	Unplanned but delivered
Skills *Balance Sheet View – Tangible Items*	Assets
	Liabilities
Style *Balance Sheet View – Intangible Items*	Attributes
	Conduct

Tool Taxonomy

General Management ▬▬

Performance Management ▬▬

Applicable Roles

Manager

Coach

129

Topgrading

A bit of employee turnover is not a bad thing – after all, half of the people in the world are below the median.

Here are three methods for identifying your best employees and clearing out the rest.

Rack and Stack. Rank all of your employees by their performance, then get rid of a certain number of your bottom performers. Hire that number of new employees. In theory, you will get a disproportionate share of the upper half.

ABC Players. There is a place for both high achieving employees who want bigger jobs, and for employees who do well but are happy with where they are. Place all of your employees into three categories – A, B and C. Keep all of your A players, get rid of all of the C players and maintain a desired ratio of A's and B's.

Top Quartile. Pay your high performers over and above what you would pay your average performers – expect them to perform in accordance with their pay scale. Hire only people from the top quartile. Hire the best and pay the best.

Tool Taxonomy

Corporate Culture

General Management

Performance Management

Applicable Roles

 Strategist

Coach

130

🖐 Touchpoints*

We live in a fast-moving society where ideas are quickly shared and forgotten. Our interactions are much smaller, but more frequent. How can your business maximize its impact in these short periods of exposure? Lean into every interaction, even the smallest 30-second one. In-the-moment, real-time actions can often be the tipping point to building a new relationship. A thousand tiny touchpoints can have a cumulative, exponential effect. The best strategy for using touchpoints is to be tough-minded and tender-hearted in the interaction. Try to make every touchpoint fit the following criteria:

- *Logical.* Appeal to the mind
- *Authentic.* Appeal to the heart
- *Competent.* Appeal to the hand

*Attributed to Doug Conant, TouchPoints

Tool Taxonomy

Human Behavior

Marketing

Applicable Roles

Preacher

Manager

131

⊞ Two Dimensions, Four Cultures*

| What kind of culture are you creating in your workplace?

This tool measures the dynamics of a business using two dimensions – sociability and solidarity – and helps you identify the sort of environment you wish to cultivate.

Sociability. Measure of a community's commitment to sincere friendliness and social interactions among the members.

Solidarity. Measure of a community's commitment to the results of the organization.

Using those two parameters, there are four cultures that could form:

Communal. (High solidarity, high sociability) Everyone is friendly to one another and works well together. Employees are focused on achieving the organization's goals. While this might seem ideal, it's difficult to fully achieve and sustain in the organization.

Networked. (High sociability, low solidarity) This is a very friendly environment, but often isn't the most efficient or productive. Employees focus on preserving more than producing. Organizations with a long-term view, where the institutional knowledge is carried in people's heads and through their relationship with each other, will find this appropriate. They cherish the long-term stability of the asset base of knowledge over the short-term benefit of deriving quick value at a cost to sociability. Examples of such organizations include research institutions, governmental departments, non-profit and volunteer groups and associations and clubs.

Mercenary. (Low sociability, high solidarity) This is a very efficient office, but not a sociable environment. This is not a country club. People are here to work; we have a job to do and we intend to win. Employees focus on producing more than preserving. Such a culture works well in companies that operate in fast-paced, competitive

Tool Taxonomy

Corporate Culture

Human Behavior

Applicable Roles

Visionary

Preacher

Strategist

132

markets. A common assumption in these organizations is that at the end of the year every individual is a year more fatigued, and that you can always find somebody else who is just as good (if not more current) that is ready to go. Most financial institutions, high-tech companies and sales organizations operate in this culture.

Fragmented. (Low sociability, low solidarity) This is an environment where individuality of work and space is cherished. The assumption in these environments is that the organization is an assembly of independent workers with common needs of support and infrastructure. Law firms, accounting firms and real estate companies should serve as good examples. Each individual intends to conduct his own business and relies little on the other professionals. Focus is more on winning for yourself than achieving a common goal. Interactions with others are cordial, but not overtly social.

There is nothing inherently right or wrong with any of these cultures. Understand which culture your company falls into, determine whether it's appropriate for the nature of your business and examine whether you're promoting values that align with that culture.

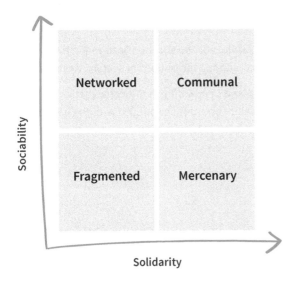

*Attributed to Rob Goff and Gareth Jones

 # Types of Conversations*

> In conversations it is good for all parties to be aligned in the objective of the conversation: do you wish to talk or do you wish to act? Each has a place, but different objectives can lead to frustration. It is useful to have a nomenclature of types of conversations so that people can be clear of their objective. We offer three types of conversations.

The Types of Conversations

Possibility. The philosophy behind this type of conversation is that uninhibited dreaming will allow others to dream too, creating an idyllic and imaginative space where new ideas and opportunities can form. There is no intention of making any evaluations or coming to a solution. The purpose is simply to dream. Pulling back from immediate evaluation will allow people to open up and venture thoughts and opinions in a scenario where they may otherwise be inhibited.

Opportunity. Evaluate the possibilities produced. The goal here is to weigh the pros and cons involved in the issue without comparing the options or seeking a resolution.

Action. This is the time to make a choice and take action. In this conversation you compare your options for action and evaluations of those options with the goal of coming to a conclusion and enacting it.

Possibility	Opportunity	Action
Brainstorm	**Weigh the Pros/Cons**	**Decision-Making**
Diffuse in nature	*Neither specific nor diffuse in nature*	*Specific in nature*

*Attributed to Glenn Mangurian

Tool Taxonomy	Applicable Roles
Human Behavior	Coach
Personal Growth	Sergeant
Team Dynamics	

Valuation of Companies

> In valuing companies, approach your valuation from multiple perspectives and triangulate on a range of values that are reasonably consistent with all of those perspectives:

Financial. Calculate revenue, profit and EBITDA. How might they continue to fare over the next few years? What multiples of those metrics do other companies command? Is there a multivariate correlation between the value other companies command and their revenue and EBITDA?

Historical. How much did you invest in this company? What is your return on investment? While this analysis is curiously amusing, the result serves no value. It is purely emotional. How much you invested, gained or lost is irrelevant to a potential buyer.

Comparative. How does your company compare to others recently bought and sold? The current market environment can cause the value of your company to fluctuate. General market conditions could be down, depressing all companies. Your particular market may be hot, creating a high demand for companies like yours. Although one might argue that it is perceived value, the value becomes real if you transact under those market conditions. Look at recent market transactions and make adjustments for the differences for your company and the transacted company.

Net present value (NPV) of free cash flow. This is probably the most reliable valuation. However, it requires a fair number of assumptions about the future. How much cash does the company generate and what does the future cash flow look like? To create a valuation, you technically need to compute the net present value (under some assumption of a discount rate) of the infinite series of future cash flow. However, more practically, it is customary to limit the cash flow assumptions to the next few (five or 10) years and substitute the tail of the infinite series with a Terminal Value. The Terminal Value dominates in this computation.

Tool Taxonomy		Applicable Roles
Business Lessons	▬▬▬	● Strategist
General Management	▬▬▬	Manager
Marketing	▬▬	

 # Value Stack

We have understood the manufacturing value chain since the industrial revolution. We are now in a data revolution.

Most companies understand how to collect **raw data**, transform it into **cleaned information** and then **draw conclusions through analysis** of that information. Companies that are succeeding and will continue to succeed understand how to use **intuition** and identify and act on **patterns**. There is a tendency to stop at analysis and never move to insight because there is a risk.

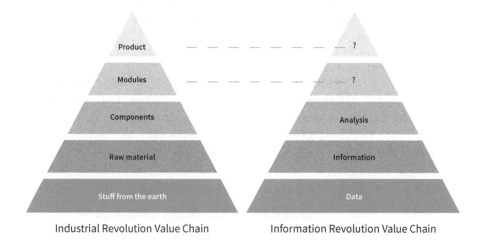

Industrial Revolution Value Chain   Information Revolution Value Chain

Designed in collaboration with Professor Timothy Clark.

Tool Taxonomy		Applicable Roles
Business Lessons	▬	Visionary
General Management	▬	Strategist
Marketing	▬	

Video Tape Test

A test for operating at the Third Bar of Integrity

When it comes to openness and transparency, are you speaking in a constructive and compassionate manner? The test is simply this: if there were a camera recording your conversation, would you be embarrassed to have the subject of your conversation watch the video? Even when the situation necessitates a private conversation, you should be operating in a spirit of respect and integrity. This can build trust and change behaviors throughout your organization.

Tool Taxonomy

Corporate Culture
Personal Growth

Applicable Roles

Preacher
Teacher
Coach

137

 Well and Fence

Situation: How does your company manage employees?
How do you keep your employees focused on what needs
to be done, to do it right, and to do it by doing right?
This Tool asks, are you building fences or digging wells?

Model:

Leaders have a stewardship responsibility for their employees and for their companies. A core component of that responsibility is keeping employees focused and aligned with the company's strategic goals.

To fulfill this responsibility, you could build "fences" to keep employees where you want them. Or, you could dig "wells" to draw your employees in and motivate them to go where you want them. In this second approach, the well becomes the center of the company.

Possible Actions:

Look at where you have built fences and where you have built wells. Share this concept with your people and identify the wells and the fences. In the course of conducting your business, introduce the vocabulary of, "is that a well or a fence?"

Tool Taxonomy		Applicable Roles
Corporate Culture	▮▮▮	Teacher
General Management	▮▮▮	Manager
		Coach

Fences:
- Rule-based
- Externally-motivated employees
- Old-school management approach
- Low cost to conceive, high cost to maintain

Wells:
- Purpose-based
- Internally-motivated employees
- New-school management approach
- High cost to conceive, low cost to maintain

What Value Do You Add?

> Determining how much value your business adds
> in the context of its supply chain can help you
> determine how much control you have over price.

To calculate how much value your business provides directly to the customer, first identify how close you are to the customer. Are you a manufacturer, master distributor, local sales representative or retail/online store? Those closest to the customer will have the most leverage.

Second, how is that value created? Is it through the tangible work that you do (income statement value) or through what/whom you know and your relationships (balance sheet value)? Typically, those with the client relationships have more leverage in determining price and assigned value.

Tool Taxonomy

General Management

Marketing

Applicable Roles

 Visionary

Manager

Worker

140

TOOL
TAXONOMY

	Corporate Culture	Marketing	Business Lessons	Personal Growth	Human Behavior	Team Dynamics	General Management	Performance Management
Abandonment		■	■				■	
Ways to Abandon		■	■					
Advice for Victims				■	■			
Affinity Mapping		■					■	
Amygdala Hijacking					■			
Analysis of Investment Portfolio		■	■				■	
Anchoring		■				■		
Archetypes of Performing Employees	■				■	■		■
Bible Thumping						■	■	
Black Swan		■	■					
Book of Tricks				■	■			
Bruce Tuckman's Model						■	■	
Category of Meetings						■		
Change Management	■							
Change Table					■			
Circle of Concern				■	■			
Co-accountability	■			■		■	■	

	Corporate Culture	Marketing	Business Lessons	Personal Growth	Human Behavior	Team Dynamics	General Management	Performance Management
Coaching through Advocacy				X	X		X	
Communicating Change: Mermaids and Alligators	X			X		X		
Conversation Meter	X					X		
Convictions vs. Conclusions	X		X					
Convolution vs. Conglomeration	X		X					
Crossing the Chasm		X	X					
Deming's Model	X			X	X			
Diminishing Returns				X				X
Disciplines of Market Leaders		X					X	
Discretionary Effort				X			X	X
Earns and Turns		X					X	
Empowerment	X				X		X	
Enthusiasm Decay				X	X			
Facts vs. Interpretations				X	X			
Fear of Empowerment				X	X		X	
Feature Creep		X	X					
Five Dysfunctions of a Team						X	X	

143

	Corporate Culture	Marketing	Business Lessons	Personal Growth	Human Behavior	Team Dynamics	General Management	Performance Management
Five Functions of a CFO							■	
Five Roles of a Board							■	
Five Temptations of a CEO				■			■	
Fixed Point Theorem						■		
Focus through Exclusion				■				
Foreground and Background Conversations				■				
Forks in the Road		■						
Four Frameworks for Leadership	■					■		
Four Types of Leverage			■					
Front of the Room vs. Back of the Room				■				
Gallery Owner's Dilemma	■							■
Give and Take				■	■			
Habit Energy				■				
Hierarchy of Intangible Assets	■					■		
Holistic Compensation Model							■	
How Level is Your Playing Field	■					■		
How Taut is Your Bungee Cord?				■		■		

144

	Corporate Culture	Marketing	Business Lessons	Personal Growth	Human Behavior	Team Dynamics	General Management	Performance Management
Implicit Assumptions				■	■			
Income Statement vs. Balance Sheet				■			■	
Inside and Outside	■					■	■	
Intensity of Presence				■				
Inverse Square Law of Conversations						■	■	
Investment Criteria		■	■					
Jack Welch's Formula	■		■					
Law of Hazard			■			■		
Law of Inertia				■	■			
Levels of Commitment					■		■	
Levels of Performance	■			■				■
Long Tail		■		■				
Loyalty	■					■	■	
Management Hierarchy						■		
Managerial Discretion					■		■	■
McKinsey's 7S Model		■					■	
Mind Those Qs				■	■			

	Corporate Culture	Marketing	Business Lessons	Personal Growth	Human Behavior	Team Dynamics	General Management	Performance Management
Nine Box Matrix			■				■	■
Nine out of Ten	■				■			■
No Pain, No Gain					■	■		
One Hundred Questions				■	■			
Open vs. Closed				■	■	■		
Parking Lot Exercise	■							■
Performing vs. Engaged	■				■			■
Personal Assets and Liabilities				■			■	
Power of the Means			■	■				■
Preference for Anonymous Harm					■	■		
Pressure vs. Stress				■	■		■	■
Pricing Models		■	■					
Principle of Externality		■	■					
Prisoner's Dilemma			■					
Progress Curve			■			■		
Quadratic Law of Conversations					■		■	
Quality of Revenue			■					

	Corporate Culture	Marketing	Business Lessons	Personal Growth	Human Behavior	Team Dynamics	General Management	Performance Management
Rational Choice Theory			■		■			
Resignation Exercise	■						■	■
Riding the Waves of Culture	■				■			
Risk Profile	■	■	■					
Rogers' Diffusion of Innovations		■					■	
Scope of Consciousness				■		■		
Signature Loop	■						■	
Simple Formula				■				
Situational Leadership						■		
Sixes and Nines	■							■
Socratic Conversations				■	■			
Specific vs. Diffuse				■		■		
Speed of Change						■		
Start With Why	■		■		■			
Stewardship	■		■					
Strategy Busting		■	■				■	
Stream of Consciousness				■	■			

147

	Corporate Culture	Marketing	Business Lessons	Personal Growth	Human Behavior	Team Dynamics	General Management	Performance Management
Supervisor/Subordinate Escalation							■	■
Talking Stick						■	■	
Test for Transparency	■				■			
Test of a Teaching Organization	■			■				
The Theory of White Space						■		
Three Bars of Integrity	■			■				■
Three Dimensions of Performance Reviews								■
Topgrading	■							■
Touchpoints		■			■			
Two Dimensions, Four Cultures	■				■			
Types of Conversations				■		■		
Valuation of Companies		■	■				■	
Value Stack		■						
Video Tape Test	■			■				
Well and Fence	■						■	
What Value Do You Add?		■					■	

APPLICABLE
ROLES

	Visionary	Preacher	Strategist	Teacher	Manager	Coach	Sergeant	Worker
Abandonment	■	■	■					
Ways to Abandon	■		■					
Advice for Victims				■		■		
Affinity Mapping			■			■		
Amygdala Hijacking						■	■	
Analysis of Investment Portfolio			■		■			
Anchoring			■	■				
Archetypes of Performing Employees					■	■		
Bible Thumping			■			■		
Black Swan	■		■					
Book of Tricks				■		■		
Bruce Tuckman's Model	■				■			
Category of Meetings					■		■	
Change Management			■		■			
Change Table	■	■						
Circle of Concern					■	■		
Co-accountability		■			■		■	

	Visionary	Preacher	Strategist	Teacher	Manager	Coach	Sergeant	Worker
Coaching through Advocacy					■	■		
Communicating Change: Mermaids and Alligators		■			■		■	
Conversation Meter		■		■				
Convictions vs. Conclusions		■		■				
Convolution vs. Conglomeration		■		■				
Crossing the Chasm	■		■					
Deming's Model				■	■			
Diminishing Returns			■					■
Disciplines of Market Leaders	■							
Discretionary Effort		■				■		■
Earns and Turns			■		■			
Empowerment	■	■			■			
Enthusiasm Decay					■	■		
Facts vs. Interpretations					■			
Fear of Empowerment		■			■			
Feature Creep			■		■			
Five Dysfunctions of a Team					■		■	

	Visionary	Preacher	Strategist	Teacher	Manager	Coach	Sergeant	Worker
Five Functions of a CFO	■							
Five Roles of a Board	■							
Five Temptations of a CEO	■	■						
Fixed Point Theorem					■		■	
Focus through Exclusion		■				■		
Foreground and Background Conversations				■	■			
Forks in the Road			■		■			
Four Frameworks for Leadership	■	■						
Four Types of Leverage			■					
Front of the Room vs. Back of the R oom	■				■			
Gallery Owner's Dilemma					■	■		
Give and Take			■					■
Habit Energy						■		■
Hierarchy of Intangible Assets	■	■						
Holistic Compensation Model			■					
How Level is Your Playing Field	■		■		■			
How Taut is Your Bungee Cord?		■			■			

	Visionary	Preacher	Strategist	Teacher	Manager	Coach	Sergeant	Worker
Implicit Assumptions			■		■	■		■
Income Statement vs. Balance Sheet	■		■	■				
Inside and Outside	■					■		
Intensity of Presence	■	■						
Inverse Square Law of Conversations					■		■	
Investment Criteria	■		■					
Jack Welch's Formula	■	■						
Law of Hazard		■	■					
Law of Inertia		■			■			
Levels of Commitment	■	■				■		
Levels of Performance					■	■		
Long Tail			■					■
Loyalty	■	■						
Management Hierarchy			■		■			
Managerial Discretion		■		■		■		
McKinsey's 7S Model			■		■			
Mind Those Qs					■	■		

	Visionary	Preacher	Strategist	Teacher	Manager	Coach	Sergeant	Worker
Nine Box Matrix			X		X			
Nine out of Ten					X	X		
No Pain, No Gain					X		X	X
One Hundred Questions				X		X		
Open vs. Closed		X		X		X		
Parking Lot Exercise					X		X	
Performing vs. Engaged					X			X
Personal Assets and Liabilities	X		X		X		X	
Power of the Means		X						
Preference for Anonymous Harm						X		
Pressure vs. Stress						X		
Pricing Models			X					
Principle of Externality	X		X					
Prisoner's Dilemma			X		X			
Progress Curve			X				X	
Quadratic Law of Conversations		X	X		X		X	
Quality of Revenue			X					

	Visionary	Preacher	Strategist	Teacher	Manager	Coach	Sergeant	Worker
Rational Choice Theory			■			■		
Resignation Exercise					■	■		
Riding the Waves of Culture	■	■	■					
Risk Profile	■	■	■					
Rogers' Diffusion of Innovations	■		■					
Scope of Consciousness	■					■		
Signature Loop	■			■				
Simple Formula	■	■				■		
Situational Leadership	■				■			
Sixes and Nines					■	■		
Socratic Conversations	■			■				
Specific vs. Diffuse			■	■		■		
Speed of Change			■		■			
Start With Why	■	■						
Stewardship					■	■		
Strategy Busting			■				■	
Stream of Consciousness			■	■				

	Visionary	Preacher	Strategist	Teacher	Manager	Coach	Sergeant	Worker
Supervisor/Subordinate Escalation					■		■	
Talking Stick				■	■	■		
Test for Transparency		■			■	■		
Test of a Teaching Organization	■			■				
The Theory of White Space					■			
Three Bars of Integrity	■	■			■			
Three Dimensions of Performance Reviews					■		■	
Topgrading			■		■	■		
Touchpoints		■			■			
Two Dimensions, Four Cultures	■	■	■					
Types of Conversations						■	■	
Valuation of Companies			■		■			
Value Stack	■							
Video Tape Test		■		■		■		
Well and Fence				■	■	■		
What Value Do You Add?	■				■			■

About Think Shift

In a world of constant change, organizations will either thrive or become irrelevant based on their ability to create and leverage that change. We help you change from the inside out.

Real change starts inside your organization, with your leadership team and employees. We deliver practical tools and advice to build intentional corporate cultures and engaged workplaces. This is the focus of our consulting team.

Successful companies are changing the way they speak with the outside world – shifting from "marketing" to "mattering." To do this, we help you create brands worth caring about, and we share them with your audiences through touchpoints worth experiencing. This is the specialty of our agency division.

This idea of change from the inside out is the foundation of everything we do at Think Shift. We don't see change as some arduous initiative or an obstacle to overcome; we believe intentional change is a powerful tool for creating opportunities that never existed before. We want to help you find and release the potential in your people, your organization, your brand. Change from the inside out means creating inspiring leaders, engaged employees and truly connected customers.

Balaji Krishnamurthy
Chairman, Think Shift

Dr. Balaji Krishnamurthy is a veteran corporate executive with more than 30 years of corporate experience, having run 16 different businesses in his career. With a Ph.D. in computer science and a strong technology background, he has run a variety of service and manufacturing based, private and public technology businesses ranging from millions of dollars to a billion dollars. As president and CEO of Planar Systems from 1999 to 2005, he led the company's transformation from a sleepy technology company to a leading player in the flat-panel display market. Even as the technology industry collapsed, annual sales of this Nasdaq high-tech company more than doubled under his watch to $256 million. *TIME* magazine recognized him as one of 25 Global Business Influentials, and national publications, such as *The Wall Street Journal,* have featured Balaji and his innovative concepts as representing a new genre of corporate leadership.

Although Balaji has five advanced degrees from prestigious institutions, his concepts of leadership are shaped from the laboratory of corporate experience rather than the classrooms of academic learning. Yet his academic training has caused him to structure his experience into practical models and tools that he has used and taught throughout his career and now teaches to corporate executives. Currently, as the chairman of Think Shift, Balaji communicates his decades of corporate leadership experience through provocative logic and passionate delivery. Known for his innovative and thought provoking concepts on corporate leadership, Balaji works with CEOs to develop organic leadership through an intentional corporate culture.